A Bibliography of Sign Languages, 2008-2017

PERMANENT INTERNATIONAL COMMITTEE OF
LINGUISTS

A Bibliography of
Sign Languages, 2008-2017

Published by the Permanent International Committee of
Linguists under the auspices of the International Council for
Philosophy and Humanistic Studies

Edited by

Anne Aarssen, René Genis & Eline van der Veken

with an introduction by

Myriam Vermeerbergen and Anna-Lena Nilsson

BRILL

LEIDEN | BOSTON

2018

The production of this book has been generously sponsored by the Stichting Bibliographie Linguistique, Leiden.

Cover illustration: A group of young people using sign language in a discussion. Photo courtesy of Andries van Niekerk, National Institute for the Deaf, South Africa, http://www.nid.org.za. Andries van Niekerk is currently working on a Dictionary of South African Sign Language.

The Library of Congress Cataloging-in-Publication Data is available online at http://catalog.loc.gov

Typeface for the Latin, Greek, and Cyrillic scripts: "Brill". See and download: brill.com/brill-typeface.

ISBN 978-90-04-37661-8 (paperback)
ISBN 978-90-04-37663-2 (e-book)

This book is printed on acid-free paper and produced in a sustainable manner.

CONTENTS*

General works

General linguistics and related disciplines

---

* Please note that this collection is a thematic extract from the *Linguistic Bibliography* annual volumes, and that certain sections falling outside of its scope were omitted.

CONTENTS

Indo-European languages

Eurasiatic languages

Languages of Mainland Southeast Asia

Sign languages

CONTENTS

INTRODUCTION

Myriam Vermeerbergen
KU Leuven & Stellenbosch University

Anna-Lena Nilsson
NTNU – Norwegian University of Science and Technology

1. Introducing signed languages

Signed languages are the natural, visual-gestural languages of Deaf communities around the world.[1] Contrary to popular belief, there is not one universal, international signed language. Even different countries that all e.g. have English as their spoken language, may have different signed languages. In the United States, for example, American Sign Language is used, in Australia the signed language is called Auslan, and in the UK the Deaf community uses British Sign Language. This indicates that signed languages have evolved independently, although there is language contact between signed and spoken languages. This is evidenced by the fact that mouth movements resembling the pronunciation of words from the surrounding spoken language seem to be an integral part of many signed languages (Boyes Braem & Sutton-Spence, 2001). In addition, there is evidence of language contact between signed languages, for example in some African countries where local and imported sign languages coexist (Nyst, 2010). There are also regional signed languages, e.g. Catalan Sign Language and Spanish Sign Language in Spain.

Signed languages were for a long time considered to be nothing but primitive systems of gestures and pantomime and therefore were believed to be more

---

1   In many countries there are actually more hearing than deaf people who know and use the national signed language, as it is also used by relatives and friends of deaf people and by people who use it in a professional capacity, e.g. signed language interpreters.

limited in what they could express than spoken languages. At the same time, signed languages are often considered to be manual versions of the ambient spoken language in a community. These somewhat paradoxical beliefs about signed languages often reside side by side. The latter view seems to be inspired by the idea that signed languages were invented by someone, to "give" to people who cannot use a spoken language. Different approaches to deaf education have resulted in an active suppression of the use of signed languages for approximately 100 years, beginning in the second half of the 19th century. Despite this, signed languages around the world have survived and continued to evolve.

Spoken and signed languages have been shown to share fundamental properties at all levels of linguistic structure. There are, however, also linguistic characteristics of signed languages that are modality specific, e.g. the use of space for linguistic purposes (Nilsson, 2008) and a (more) simultaneous organisation (Vermeerbergen, Leeson & Crasborn, 2007). The transmission of signed languages from one generation to the next also differs from that of spoken languages. Since the majority of deaf children are born to hearing (most often nonsigning parents) they usually do not start early signed language acquisition in their homes.

2. Signed language linguistics: Historical context

2.1. The start of modern signed language linguistics: The early years

For a long time, misconceptions about signed languages were also shared by the scientific community, including scholars in the field of linguistics (cf. Sapir, 1921 and Myklebust, 1957, in Armstrong & Karchmer, 2009). Signed languages were not considered genuine natural languages, and they were generally ignored in linguistic research. Signed language linguistics is thus a relatively young field of study, pioneered by Tervoort's (1953) doctoral dissertation documenting the signing of deaf children in the Netherlands and Stokoe's (1960) description of the linguistic structure of American Sign Language. During the 1960s and 1970s, other, initially mainly American, researchers began to express an interest in the linguistic structure of signs and signed language(s). In 1968, an article reporting on Tervoort's doctoral study was published in *Lingua* (Tervoort, 1968) and in 1975, two articles on American Sign Language were published in *Language* (Friedman, 1975 & Frishberg, 1975).

Towards the second half of the 1970s, several linguists in other (mainly European) countries also began to study their local signed languages. It is often assumed that this arose as a result of research on American Sign Language, but personal communication with some of these European pioneers has revealed that this was not the case. Instead, at least in some countries, there seemed to be a link between the start of signed language linguistics and renewed interest in the use of signs/signed languages in deaf education (Vermeerbergen & Leeson, 2011). *Sign Language Studies*, the first dedicated journal was launched as early as 1972, edited by William Stokoe.[2] The very first international symposium on signed language research was organised in Skepparholmen, Sweden in June 1979. Twenty out of the 26 papers presented at the conference appeared in the proceedings (Ahlgren & Bergman, 1980). Eight of these 20 papers were presented by American scholars, and 12 papers were by European scholars, of which five were from a Scandinavian country and five were from the UK. Most of the chapters in these proceedings do not present a linguistic analysis of a signed language, but rather discuss the acquisition of signs or a signed language or concern a form of sign supported speech ("Signed Danish", "Signed German", etc.)[3] rather than the national signed language proper, or they consider one or more aspect of methodology in signed language research. Although there were some universities where there was a signed language group or lab already in the 1970s, many pioneering signed language researchers worked on their own. This is likely to have made international scientific meetings even more important, as it offered opportunities for the exchange of ideas and for collaboration. We may also note here that the signed language research groups or labs that did exist often were not situated within a linguistics department, but rather affiliated with educational departments or departments of audiology/speech therapy.

The second *International Symposium on Sign Language Research* was organised two years later, in Bristol in the UK, and in the next year, 1982, the first *European Congress on Sign Language Research* was organised in Brussels. The first *Theoretical Issues in Sign Language Research* conference was held in Rochester, USA, in 1986. In the same year, ISLA, the International Sign Linguistics Association, was founded. It was based in the UK, as "a network of

---

2 Early sign language linguistics work was sometimes published in American Annals of the Deaf (e.g. Tervoort 1961), a professional journal "dedicated to quality in education and related services for deaf or hard of hearing children and adults" (http://gupress.gallaudet.edu/annals), first published in 1847.

3 Sign supported speech, also known as "simultaneous communication" or "sign systems" started to be developed in the 1960s and 1970s mainly for use in deaf education. Signs, often taken from the national signed language, are produced simultaneously with the national spoken language. The morpho-syntactic system of the spoken language is usually expressed via newly constructed manual signs.

researchers interested in aspects of sign language studies" with the principal aim to "facilitate production, dissemination and discussion of both theoretical and applied ideas within a sign linguistics framework" (Brennan & Turner, 1994:vi).

Proceedings or selected papers were published for most of these early international and European conferences. Needless to say, these volumes were very important for the signed language linguistic community at the time. Today, they offer an insight into the research community, research topics and questions, and the theoretical approaches that were prevalent then. One observation we can make is that, especially from the 1980s onwards, there was an increase in international collaboration. In some cases, this resulted in cross-linguistic studies involving two or more signed languages, although the majority of the studies remained focused on one single signed language. A second important observation concerns the broad range of topics and themes addressed during this period, including, for example, the lexicon, sociolinguistic variation, the different levels of linguistic description (phonology, morphology, syntax), non-manual behaviour, signed language learning and teaching, (bi-modal) bilingualism, signed language acquisition, signed language emergence and home signing, psycholinguistics, aspects of the Deaf community and culture, history, literature, methodological issues, etc.

An important research focus during this early period consisted in the comparison of spoken languages and signed languages, and approaches to the analysis of the latter. Karlsson (1984) discusses two very different approaches to signed language analysis, which he labels the "oral language compatibility view" and the "sign language differential view". The compatibility view presupposes that most of the characteristics of signed language structure align with what is typically described for spoken languages (i.e. oral languages), and that the approach to the analysis of signed languages can, and even should, be modelled on spoken language research. The differential view suggests that signed languages are so unique in structure that their description should not be modelled on spoken language analogies. Although in the first decades of signed language research the latter approach was clearly also present (e.g. Cuxac, 1985, 1987; DeMatteo, 1977), the majority of researchers adopted the "compatibility view". There are several reasons for this, the main of which being that signed language researchers wanted – or even needed – to provide evidence that signed languages were indeed fully-fledged, genuine languages, worthy of linguistic study in their own right. This was mostly done by demonstrating parallels between signed and spoken language grammar and structure (Vermeerbergen 2006). Much of the work on signed languages from the 1970s to the 1990s was primarily descriptive in nature, or assumed a generative framework, with relatively few exceptions (Cormier, Schembri & Woll, 2013).

To conclude this section on the early development of the field, we would like to note that early work was not always published internationally, as researchers also published in their own (written) languages, as in the case of research reports and master's or PhD theses. There was also a need for easily accessible information on the national signed language for the local Deaf community and those working with that community. Considerations like these made researchers sometimes focus on publishing in the local/national written language.

2.2.   From 1985 till 2007: A snapshot

Focusing on different approaches to the universality of signed languages, Woll (2003) distinguishes a modern and a post-modern period in signed language research, with the post-modern period starting around 1985. Where it was generally claimed that signed languages "differ substantially from each other and are mutually unintelligible" (ibid., p. 20), in the modern period, (early) cross-linguistic comparisons indicated that signed languages might resemble each other more closely than spoken languages. Early observations of common grammatical features across signed languages were related to the fact that, from the 1980s onwards, more and more signed languages were being studied, although still mainly limited to North America, Australia, and Western Europe. The observation that signed languages seemed to be typologically more homogeneous than spoken languages was frequently associated with specific properties of the visual-gestural modality. More recently, there has been an increasing interest in comparative studies that also include non-Western signed languages (Perniss, Pfau & Steinbach, 2007).

Starting from the second half of the 1980s, i.e. the post-modern period, ideas regarding the relation between spoken and signed language studies have gradually changed. Signed language studies are moving away from a description of signed languages as essentially analogous to spoken languages, and we see a growing interest in the properties that are typical of (although not always unique to) signed languages (Vermeerbergen, 2006). Examples are the use of space (Engberg-Pedersen, 1993; Nilsson, 2004, 2007; Perniss, 2007), simultaneity (Miller, 1994) and iconicity/visual imagery (Taub, 2001).

There was also increased consideration of similarities between signed languages and co-speech gesture, which both are expressed through the visual-gestural modality. Because early work on signed languages emphasized their linguistic nature, the presence of gesture in signed language use was not considered. Then the idea that gesture may be combined with signs was considered but generally discarded. The consensus seemed to have been that in signed languages, gesture either moves away from the manual channel (and may "move" to the mouth, e.g. Sandler, 2003) and/or it loses its true gestural character and becomes part of the linguistic system, e.g. McNeill, 1993 (Vermeerbergen & Demey, 2007). However, several studies after the year 2000 explore the possible presence of gesture in signed language structure, and recent analyses support a model of signed language structure that incorporates both linguistic and gestural (also called "non-linguistic", in the sense of gradient and non-conventional) elements (e.g. Liddell, 2003; Schembri, 2001; Schembri, Jones & Burnham, 2005; Vermeerbergen & Demey, 2007, amongst others).

This new perspective led to the revision of some earlier interpretations of signed language structure, e.g. with regard to so-called "classifier constructions" (Vermeerbergen & Van Herreweghe, 2010). Early analysis of classifier constructions in signed languages often made comparisons to the classificatory verbs in Athapaskan languages. Early descriptions suggested that the component parts of these constructions were discrete, listable and specified in the grammar of individual signed languages, each having morphemic status (e.g. Supalla 1982). More recent studies, often using the term "depicting signs", instead considered the possibility of dealing with these constructions as mixed forms, i.e. structures involving both linguistic and "non-linguistic components" (e.g. Liddell, 2003; Schembri, Jones & Burnham, 2005), which align with earlier work by Cogill-Koez (2000), who argued that a "classifier construction" was a visual representation of an action, event, or spatial relationship rather than a lexical or a productive sign.

Research on pointing actions has also revealed interesting parallels between pointing gestures and pointing signs (Liddell, 2000; Vermeerbergen & Demey, 2007), and work on constructed action, also called enactment, i.e. the use of bodily movements, postures and eye gaze to construct actions and dialogue in order to show characters, events and points of view, showed how signers habitually integrate elements of showing into their signing (Metzger, 1995; Liddell & Metzger 1998; Liddell, 2003; Quinto-Pozos, 2007).

A growing number of researchers began to propose that signed languages be analysed as heterogeneous systems in which meanings are conveyed by using a combination of elements, rather than as homogeneous systems where all major elements of signing behaviour are considered to be equal parts of a morphosyntactic system (e.g., Schembri 2001; Liddell, 2003). Emerging from this strand of research was the idea that when the communication of signers and speakers is compared, speech plus co-speech gesture rather than speech alone should be considered as an equivalent to signing (Vermeerbergen & Demey, 2007). Both speakers and signers coordinate different articulators and convey information by producing composite multi-modal expressions to convey information.

With respect to publications during this period, we may note the following developments:

1. The publication of journals and periodicals in languages other than English. In France for example, from 1977 till 1987, *Coup d'Oeil* was published. In the Netherlands, from 1986 onwards (probably until 1992), *GebaarEnNieuws* was published, a newsletter in written Dutch mainly aimed at the national Deaf community. In Germany, *Das Zeichen* was established in 1987. It still exists today (June 2018) as the only journal on the topic of signed languages and Deaf communities in the area of German-speaking countries.

2. The publication of the first International Bibliography of Sign Language, in 1993 (Joachim & Prillwitz, 1993).

3. The launch of a new international journal, focusing on signed language linguistic research, called *Sign Language & Linguistics* in 1998.

4. Publication of a number of descriptions of (parts of) the grammar of different signed languages, often in the national written language (e.g. Prillwitz & Leven, 1985, for German Sign Language; Schermer, Fortgens, Harder & de Nobel, 1990, for Sign Language of the Netherlands; Pilleux, Cuevas, & Avalos, 1991, for Spanish Sign Language; Dubuisson & Nadeau, 1993, for Quebec Sign Language; Moody, 1993, for French Sign Language; Vermeerbergen, 1996, for Flemish Sign Language; Malmquist & Mosand, 1996, for Norwegian Sign Language; and Ahlgren & Bergman, 2006, for Swedish Sign Language).

5. In some countries, (partial) grammars were also produced in the form of a so-called "signing book", i.e. a publication in a signed language, recorded on video or (later) CD-ROM (see also Section 4).

6. Books, and especially edited volumes, continued to be important for dissemination of research results.

3. The last decade: Most recent trends and developments

Over the past recent decades, the field of signed language linguistics has expanded considerably. With this growth, and the specialisation into subfields, it has become increasingly difficult to keep track of everything that is going on. Where there was once a single dedicated journal, there are now several, and work on signed language linguistics is also more readily accepted for publication in journals and (edited) books with a much broader scope. There are also a number of specialised series, dedicated to a specific subfield or theme, e.g. the *Sociolinguistics in Deaf Communities series* (Gallaudet University Press), the

Sign Language Typology series, and the *Sign Language and Deaf Communities series* (both published by De Gruyter). Increasingly, volumes focusing on signed languages are included in book series previously dealing with spoken language linguistics only. Another indication that the field is becoming more established is the publication of extensive international handbooks on signed language linguistics, such as Pfau, Steinbach and Woll (2012). Additionally, chapters on signed languages are increasingly being included in more general handbooks, e.g. Guendouzi, Loncke & Williams (2010), Narrog & Heine (2011), and Enfield, Kockelman & Sidnell (2014). Rather than attempting to cover all aspects of the field, this section will focus on three of the more prominent developments influencing signed language linguistics during the most recent decade.[4]

3.1. Increasing number of signed languages studied

One important direction in which the field is growing, concerns the number of signed languages being described. There are now descriptions (albeit partial) available for many more national signed languages than was previously the case, and from more parts of the world. In addition, we see an increase in descriptions of so called "village sign languages", which are local indigenous signed languages used in areas with high incidences of congenital deafness (Meir, Sandler, Padden & Aronoff, 2010). In such areas, it is common that a large proportion of the hearing people living in the community can also use the signed language for communication. Examples of village signed languages include Adamorobe Sign Language (Nyst, 2007), Kata Kolok (De Vos, 2012) and Yucatec Maya Sign Language (Johnson, 1991; Le Guen, 2012).

We now also see more work on the specific characteristics of what is known as International Sign (IS) (e.g. Rosenstock & Napier, 2015). IS is a contact variety that is used for cross-linguistic communication between users of different signed languages. It is used in a number of different contexts, particularly at international meetings such as the World Federation of the Deaf Congress, and events such as the Deaflympics. IS is not as conventionalised or complex as natural signed languages. However, there is an accreditation system in place for International Sign interpreters.[5]

---

4   We may note here that some of the developments we describe started before 2007, but they have increased in importance in the last decade.

5   https://wfdeaf.org/our-work/wfd-wasli-international-sign-interpreter-accreditation/ (Accessed 20 April, 2018.)

As more and more signed languages are being described, comparative studies on signed languages that include less studied (non-Western) signed language become possible (Schwager & Zeshan, 2008; Lepic, Börstell, Belsitzman & Sandler, 2016), and it is gradually becoming easier to engage in larger-scale typological research (Zeshan & Perniss, 2008, as well as other volumes in the *Sign Language Typology* series).

When previously un-described (or under-described) signed languages are described, the researcher(s) involved may come across linguistic structures and mechanisms that were already documented for other signed languages, in some cases quite some time ago. Especially if the early publications are not (or no longer) easily available, there is a risk that older work is overlooked. And as the field – and the number of publications within the field – continues to grow, it becomes more and more difficult to keep track of all that has been published.

3.2. Contemporary approaches to signed language linguistics: specialising across sub-disciplines

Whereas much (but not all[6]) of the early signed language linguistic work was done within a structural or generative framework that was highly influential at the time, the field of signed language linguistics has continued to evolve in line with the field of linguistics in general. Today, rule-based approaches co-exist with meaning-based and usage-based approaches, as promoted within for example cognitive linguistics and functional approaches. There is also work being done with construction grammar, and a growing methodological interest in actual language use, which links up with the field of corpus linguistics (Geeraerts, 2003).

The specific ways in which the field has developed and broadened, which includes researchers becoming increasingly specialised in their work, is currently noticeable also in e.g. the more specialised conferences that are organised. Just as *Sign Language Studies* used to be "the" journal to publish in, "the" conference for signed language linguists for a long period of time was *Theoretical Issues in Sign Language Research* (*TISLR*). Now, we are witnessing a diversification with new conferences focusing on a number of topics. There is, for example, a series of conferences devoted to signed language acquisition, in a very broad sense, with the 3rd *International Conference on Sign Language Acquisition* (ICSLA) taking place in 2018 (http://www.icsla2018.com/). There is also a series of yearly

---

6   Early work also includes e.g. sociolinguistic studies on variation, mainly lexical variation, often with a lexicographic purpose.

conferences for researchers doing formal and experimental research on signed languages: *FEAST*, which is short for *Formal and Experimental Advances in Sign language Theory*. This has also resulted in the electronic, open access *FEAST Journal:* http://www.raco.cat/index.php/FEAST. The most recent addition to the field is the first international workshop on cognitive and functional explorations in signed language linguistics, *Sign CAFÉ 1*, to be held in the summer of 2018 (https://www.birmingham.ac.uk/schools/edacs/departments/englishlanguage/events/2018/sign-cafe.aspx).

While it is indeed clear that within the domain of signed language linguistics more and more specialisation is taking place, it is still important for many researchers to remain acquainted with and engage in a wide range of research. For example, in some countries there are still very few signed language researchers (or even only one), and it may be necessary for them to engage in many different types of research/activities, resulting in the researcher not being able to specialise. The societal relevance of signed language research, including the need for information on the linguistics of specific signed languages as well as the need for signed language teaching and signed language interpreter training, certainly also plays a role here. The following comment from Brennan (1986: 16) is still relevant:

> "The needs and demands of those wishing to learn sign language are possibly the most pressing of the influences affecting us today. It is hard to focus on, for example, the most linguistically efficient abstract representation of simultaneous patterning within the word when people are crying out for basic information on the grammar of sign."

Societal needs may also result in researchers publishing their work locally, in the national language, and/or invest a lot of time in dissemination activities directed towards the local Deaf community. Nevertheless, as signed language linguists we also have a responsibility to make our work known to other linguists – and beyond the field.

3.3. Technological advances

Early signed language researchers faced specific problems due to the lack of a widely accepted writing system for signed languages and limitations in the technologies available to them. Early signed language data were video-recorded on tape, using analogue video cameras. Transcription was initially done with pencil and paper, while viewing the recorded data with the help of a video player that would, at best, be equipped with a remote control and the possibility to view the recording in slow motion.

In the past, any set of data on which a linguistic analysis was performed was called a "corpus". Fortunately, the advent of digitized video-recordings, computer technology and software development has made it possible to build substantial signed language corpora. Signed language corpora consist of large amounts of annotated texts in a machine-readable form, which aims to be maximally representative of the language and its users and can be consulted to study the type and frequency of constructions in a language (Johnston & Schembri, 2013; Fenlon, Schembri, Johnston & Cormier, 2015). This is an important development, as the previous reliance on small sets of data and/or the intuitions of only few informants is problematic, especially in view of the fact that signed language use is highly variable (Johnston & Schembri, 2013).

The first modern signed language corpus projects began in 2004 in Australia and in Ireland, soon followed by a number of similar projects for other European signed languages, e.g. Sign Language of the Netherlands, British Sign Language, German Sign Language, and Swedish Sign Language.[7]

The first stage in building a corpus is to collect data and convert these into a digital video archive. The Auslan Corpus, for example, contains approximately 300 hours of digital video recordings of naturalistic signing, by 255 native or near-native deaf participants, edited into approximately 1,100 video clips suitable for detailed annotation (Johnston, 2008).

In the next stage, annotation work is undertaken, and the digital video archive is transformed into a modern linguistic corpus. Johnston (2010) stresses that in order for the dataset to become machine-readable and searchable, two types of annotation are essential: ID glossing and a translation into one or more written languages. Annotation of signed language corpora is often done using the open-source computer software ELAN, developed by the Max Planck Institute for Psycholinguistics (MPI) in Nijmegen, the Netherlands (Crasborn and Sloetjes, 2008). All existing signed language corpora are currently in the process of undergoing linguistic annotation or are awaiting annotation.

---

7 Almost ten years before, Ceil Lucas, Robert Bayley, and their team collected a large-scale corpus of American Sign Language (e.g. Lucas, Bayley & Valli, 2001). Their work clearly inspired later signed language corpus projects, but that corpus is not considered to be one of the modern signed language corpora, mainly because it has not been appropriately annotated and is thus not machine-readable.

INTRODUCTION

When collecting a corpus, it is of the utmost importance to also collect and store metadata related to the linguistic data gathered. In many recent projects, the *IMDI metadata database* is being used, an already existing database which has been further developed in the context of the *ECHO project* at the Max Planck Institute for Psycholinguistics in Nijmegen (The Netherlands) (Crasborn & Hanke 2003; also see www.mpi.nl/IMDI/).

Corpora are often built for linguistic research, but the data can also be used for the preservation of older signed language data for future research (i.e. the documentation of diachronic change) or as authentic materials to be used in signed language teaching. Johnston (2008, 82) expresses the need for signed language corpora as follows:

> "Signed language corpora will vastly improve peer review of descriptions of signed languages and make possible, for the first time, a corpus-based approach to signed language analysis. Corpora are important for the testing of language hypotheses in all language research at all levels, from phonology through to discourse (…). This is especially true of deaf signing communities which are also inevitably young minority language communities. Although introspection and observation can help develop hypotheses regarding language use and structure, because signed languages lack written forms and well developed community-wide standards, and have interrupted transmission and few native speakers, intuitions and researcher observations may fail in the absence of clear native signer consensus of phonological or grammatical typicality, markedness or acceptability. The past reliance on the intuitions of very few informants and isolated textual examples (which have remained essentially inaccessible to peer review) has been problematic in the field. Research into signed languages has grown dramatically over the past three to four decades but progress in the field has been hindered by the resulting obstacles to data sharing and processing."

In the last decade, a series of workshops and other international scientific meetings were (and are being) organised to combine and share expertise in signed language corpus development and to promote international cooperation. During these meetings participants discuss data collection, technical formats, organisation of metadata, annotation processes, as well as questions of accessibility, dissemination and use of signed language data. A number of publications results from such meetings, e.g. Dreuw, et al. (2010) and Crasborn, et al. (2012), the latter specifically dealing with the interface of corpus and lexical databases. Indeed, often, the creation of a signed language corpus goes hand in hand with the development of lexical database, which may in turn be used to create online dictionaries (e.g. the British Sign Language SignBank (Fenlon et al. 2014) and BSL SignBank Dictionary (http://bslsignbank.ucl.ac.uk/about/dictionary/).

Finally, another change that has been brought about by technological advances relates to illustrations included in or accompanying publications. With digital video files and new computer software, it is now easy (and cheap) to include a large number of photo illustrations in journals and books. Also, printed books may have an accompanying DVD with filmed examples or a website containing even more video clips. There are, of course, also more and more digital web-based publications that allow the inclusion of video-based examples.

4. The position of signed languages and deaf scholars in signed language linguistics

In the first sentence of this introduction we described signed languages as the languages of Deaf communities. In this concluding section, we would like to discuss the position of deaf people, deaf scholars and signed languages within signed language linguistics. The majority of pioneering researchers were hearing linguists, who were late L2 learners of the signed language they studied, and some had only limited signing skills.[8] Often, deaf informants and/or research assistants were engaged to help with data collection, annotation and analysis. At the time, academic training was not readily accessible for deaf members of research teams, e.g. because they did not meet the admission requirements and/or because there were no possibilities to have interpreters in education.

Currently many signed language researchers have good language proficiency levels in the signed language they are studying and working on. There are also signed language linguists who have acquired a signed language as their first language, both hearing and deaf, and these researchers with native signing skills bring an important perspective to the field. The number of deaf researchers within the field of signed language linguistics is, however, still rather limited, especially at postgraduate level. This continues to be related to educational opportunities, including the difficulties faced by deaf students regarding access to higher education. Even where higher education is or has been possible, it is still not easy for deaf academics to push through to higher positions. (Kusters, De Meulder & O'Brien, 2017).

---

8   This is related to the fact that in many countries opportunities for formal learning of signed languages were very limited or even non-existent.

INTRODUCTION

In 1996-97, Kyle and Allsop conducted a review of the status of European signed languages. They found a striking disparity between content written about Deaf communities and what material Deaf communities themselves had access to in their own languages (Kyle & Allsop, 1997). Since 2002 there are international conferences specifically targeting deaf academics, organized by the Deaf Academics organization. One of the aims of the *Deaf Academics Conferences* is to gain a better understanding of the issues that they face in the academic environment (http://dac2017.com/about/). Such conferences are video-recorded but do not often find their way into print and they are not always accessible to hearing (non-signing) researchers (Kusters, De Meulder and O' Brien, 2017).

Signed languages do not have written forms, and experiments with the development of a writing system (e.g. SignWriting) has had only limited success. In the 1990s, technological developments, especially in the field of digital video, made it possible to video-record longer texts in a signed language for dissemination by means of video cassettes or later CDs and DVDs. From the second half of the 1990s onwards, there were some experiments producing so-called "signing books" (cf. the European "signing books project"), e.g. (partial) reference grammars or other linguistic texts targeting Deaf communities members (e.g. Vermeerbergen, 1999). Some universities also offered deaf students the opportunity to produce papers in the national signed language, including master dissertations and sometimes, but to a lesser extent, doctoral theses. However, such practices have not become widespread.

In addition, English remains the primary language of the academy, and this significantly affects the functional employment of signed languages by students of signed languages and deaf academics. A pilot study carried out in Belgium and Ireland in 2013 explored how students and academics create and use signed materials (Leeson, Sheikh & Vermeerbergen, 2015). There, one Irish deaf academic noted that he and his colleagues present their own academic work at conferences in a signed language, but they prefer to prepare publishable data in English even when they may feel less confident about their skills in written English. Just as in Ireland, the Flemish informants reported that when offered the opportunity to hand in (student) work presented in a signed language, they did not avail themselves of this option for several reasons (Leeson, Sheikh, & Vermeerbergen, 2015:178):

1. They were not used to using a signed language for academic purposes and/ or were used to using English for academic writing (more so than Dutch, their primary "spoken" language).

2. They said that writing (in English) allows one to go back, reread, rewrite, and restructure, but they felt that this is not possible in a signed language text.
3. They felt that no clear guidelines exist on how to produce a paper in a signed language. For example, how do you handle notes, and how do you present a bibliography?
4. They argued that creating a signed text is very time consuming.

As with the deaf Irish academics, deaf Flemish academics pointed out that they like being able to present in a signed language, e.g., at conferences. These informants also referred to the *Deaf Studies Digital Journal*[9] and acknowledged the important role that that journal may play in further developing academic registers in signed languages.

Kusters, De Meulder & O'Brien (2017: 32), who discuss deaf scholars' positions in academic settings, note the following:

> "Publication in signed languages (such as in the online Deaf Studies Digital Journal or on DVD published by Ishara Press) are not always the solution, because even those deaf scholars who are fluent in sign languages do not always master and often have not been trained in using the appropriate academic register. Furthermore, the academic impact of these appearances is lower than for printed journals (…). In addition, publishing in English is necessary in order to contribute to other disciplines."

And yet, especially with a view to getting information across to Deaf communities, dissemination in a signed language remains important.

5. Conclusion

Signed language linguistics is still a young field of study, with the start of modern signed language linguistics happening only about fifty years ago. Looking back on the past decades clearly shows that the field has travelled an important distance in a relatively short period of time. In this introduction we explained that early research often focused on demonstrating that signed languages were

---

9 The Deaf Studies Digital Journal is published by Gallaudet University, the first issue appeared in 2009.

indeed full, complex, independent languages. Such studies emphasised the similarities between signed and spoken languages, on the one hand, and the differences between signed languages and gesture on the other. In later years, research has turned more towards the modality-specific properties of signed languages, comparing different (related and unrelated) signed languages, and there has also been an increasing interest in comparing aspects of signed languages to gestural aspects of spoken communication. Furthermore, we have pointed out that theoretical developments and advances within the field of spoken language linguistics can also be found in signed language studies. We also showed how new technologies and tools facilitate, for example, the construction of large-scale, machine-readable signed language corpora, which offer opportunities to address new research questions.

Indeed, as more and more signed language corpus data are being annotated, a process that has proven to be extremely labour-intensive, exciting new developments occur. In the near future, we may expect more elaborate linguistic descriptions of individual signed languages, larger-scale socio-linguistic studies, international collaboration in cross-linguistic and typological studies, as well as research and development towards automatic sign recognition and signed language machine translation.

Looking forward, we also expect to see signed language and spoken language research and gesture studies increasingly approaching each other. Today, even though not all linguists are equally convinced of the linguistic status of signed languages, linguistic research into signed languages is a part of many linguistic sub-disciplines. At the same time, it is more and more accepted that the study of gestures will lead to a greater understanding of natural languages and human communication. Gesture researchers and signed language researchers also increasingly meet at workshops and conferences, addressing issues of common interest.

As the division between research on spoken languages, signed languages, and gesture continues to diminish, studying human communication and interaction from a multi-modal perspective may lead to important new insights within the field of linguistics, facilitating a comparative semiotics of diverse language practices (e.g., Enfield, 2009; Kendon, 2014; Green, Kelly & Schembri, 2014; Ferrara & Hodge, 2018). After all, human communication primarily is a multi-modal activity.

References

Ahlgren, Inger, & Bergman, Brita (Eds.). (1980). *Papers from the First International Symposium on Sign Language Research. June 10-16, 1979 Skepparholmen, Sweden.* Leksand: Sveriges Dövas Riksförbund.

Ahlgren, Inger, & Bergman, Brita. (2006). Det svenska teckenspråket. In: *Teckenspråk och teckenspråkiga. Kunskaps- och forskningsöversikt. SOU 2006:29* (pp. 11-70). Stockholm: Socialdepartementet. [Swedish Sign Language. In: *Sign Language and Signing People. Summary of Research and Knowledge Status.*]

Armstrong, David F., & Karchmer, Michael A. (2009). William C. Stokoe and the Study of Signed Languages. *Sign Language Studies* 9(4) (Summer 2009), 389-397.

Brennan, Mary. (1986). Linguistic Perspectives. In: Bernard T. Tervoort (Ed.): *Signs of life. Proceedings of the Second European Congress on Sign Language Research, Amsterdam July 14-18, 1985* (pp. 1-16). Amsterdam: Univ. of Amsterdam.

Brennan, Mary, & Turner, Graham H. (1994). Preface. In: Mary Brennan & Graham H. Turner (Eds.). *Issues in Sign Language. Working Papers* (pp. VI-VII) Durham: ISLA.

Boyes Braem, Penny, & Sutton-Spence, Rachel (Eds.). (2001). *The hands are the head of the mouth: The mouth as articulator in sign language.* Hamburg: Signum Verlag.

Cogill-Koez, Dorothy. (2000). Signed language classifier predicates: linguistic structures or schematic visual representation? *Sign Language and Linguistics, 3*(2), 153-207.

Cormier, Kearsy, Schembri, Adam, & Woll, Bencie. (2013). Pronouns and pointing in sign languages. *Lingua 137*, 230-247.

Crasborn, Onno, Efthimiou, Eleni, Fotinea, Evita, Hanke, Thomas, Kristoffersen, Jette, & Mesch, Johanna (Eds.). (2012). *Workshop proceedings: 5th Workshop on the Representation and Processing of Sign Languages: Interactions between corpus and lexicon: 8th International Conference on Language Resources and Evaluation, LREC 2012, Istanbul.* Paris: European Language Resources Association.

Crasborn, Onno, & Hanke, Thomas. (2003). *Additions to the IMDI Metadata Set for Sign Language Corpora. Agreements at an ECHO workshop, May 2003, Nijmegen University.* www.ru.nl/publish/pages/522090/signmetadata_oct2003.pdf.

Crasborn, Onno, & Sloetjes, Han. (2008). Enhanced ELAN functionality for sign language corpora. In: Onno Crasborn, Eleni Efthimiou, Thomas Hanke,

INTRODUCTION

Ernst D. Thoutenhoofd, & Inge Zwitserlood (Eds.). *The third workshop on the representation and processing of sign languages: Construction and exploitation of sign language corpora* [*a workshop given at the Sixth International Conference on Language Resources and Evaluation, 26 May – 1 June 2008, Marrakech, Morocco* (pp. 39-43). Paris: European Language Resources Association.

Cuxac, Christian. (1985). Esquisse d'une typologie des langues des signes. In: Christian Cuxac (Ed.). *Autour de la langue des signes, Journées d'Études 10* (pp. 35-60). Paris: UFR de linguistique générale et appliquée, Université René Descartes.

Cuxac, Christian. (1987). Transitivité en langue des signes (LSF). Structures de l'iconicité. In: D. François-Geiger (org.). *La transitivité et ses corrélats* (cycle de conférences) (pp. 15-49). Paris: Centre de Linguistique, Travaux n° 1, Université René Descartes.

DeMatteo, Asa (1977). Visual imagery and visual analogues. In: Lynn A. Friedman (Ed). *On the Other Hand: Recent Perspectives on American Sign Language* (pp. 109-136). New York: Academic Press.

de Vos, Connie. (2012). *Sign-Spatiality in Kata Kolok: how a village sign language of Bali inscribes its signing space.* PhD Dissertation. Nijmegen: Radboud University.

Dreuw, Philippe, Efthimiou, Eleni, Hanke, Thomas, Johnston, Trevor, Martínez Ruiz, Gregorio, & Schembri, Adam (Eds.). (2010). *Workshop proceedings: 4th Workshop on the Representation and Processing of Sign Languages: Corpora and sign language technologies: 7th International Conference on Language Resources and Evaluation, LREC 2010, Valletta.* Paris: European Language Resources Association.

Dubuisson, Colette, & Nadeau, Marie. (1993). *Etudes sur la Langue des Signes Québécoise.* Les Presses de l'Université de Montreal.

Enfield, Nick J. (2009). *The anatomy of meaning: Speech, gesture, and composite utterances.* Cambridge: Cambridge University Press.

Enfield, Nick J., Kockelman, Paul, & Sidnell, Jack. (2014). *The Cambridge handbook of linguistic anthropology.* Cambridge, UK: Cambridge Univ. Press.

Engberg-Pedersen, Elisabeth. (1993). *Space in Danish Sign Language. The Semantics and Morphosyntax of the Use of Space in a Visual Language.* Hamburg: Signum Verlag.

Fenlon, Jordan, Cormier, Kearsy, Rentelis, Ramas, Schembri, Adam, Rowley, Katherine, Adam, Robert, & Woll, Bencie. (2014). *BSL SignBank: A lexical database of British Sign Language.* London: Deafness, Cognition and Language Research Centre, Univ. College London.

Fenlon, Jordan, Schembri, Adam, Johnston, Trevor, & Cormier, Kearsy. (2015). Documentary and corpus approaches to sign language research. In: Eleni Orfanidou, Bencie Woll & Gary Morgan (Eds.). *The Blackwell Guide to Research Methods in Sign Language Studies* (pp. 156-172). Oxford: Blackwell.

Ferrara, Lindsay N., & Hodge, Gabrielle. (in press). Language as Description, Indication, and Depiction. *Frontiers in Psychology.*

Friedman, Lynn A. (1975). Space, Time, and Person Reference in American Sign Language. *Language, 51*(4), 940-961.

Frishberg, Nancy. (1975). Arbitrariness and iconicity: Historical change in American Sign Language. *Language, 51*(3), 676-710.

Geeraerts, Dirk. (2003). Decontextualizing and recontextualizing tendencies in 20th-century linguistics and literary theory. In: Ewald Mengel, Hans-Joerg Schmid, & Michael Steppat (Eds.). *Anglistentag 2002 Bayreuth* (pp. 369-379). Trier: Wissenschaftlicher Verlag.

Green, Jennifer, Kelly, Barbara F., & Schembri, Adam. (2014). Finding Common Ground: Sign Language and Gesture Research in Australia. *Australian Journal of Linguistics, 34*(2), 185-192.

Guendouzi, Jackie, Loncke, Filip, & Williams, Mandy, J. (Eds.). (2010). *The Handbook of Psycholinguistic & Cognitive processes. Perspectives in Communication Disorders.* London: Taylor & Francis Books.

Joachim, Guido, & Prillwitz, Siegmund. (1993). *International Bibliography of Sign Language.* Hamburg: Signum Verlag.

Johnson, Robert E. (1991). Sign language, culture & community in a traditional Yucatec Maya village. *Sign Language Studies 73*, 461-474.

Johnston, Trevor. (2008). Corpus Linguistics and Signed Languages: No Lemmata, No Corpus. Paper Presented at the 3rd Workshop on the Representation and Processing of Sign Languages (LREC), Marrakech, Morocco, May 2008 [http://www.lrec-conf.org/proceedings/lrec2008/, 82–87].

Johnston, Trevor. (2010). From archive to corpus: Transcription and annotation in the creation of signed language corpora. *International Journal of Corpus Linguistics 15*(1), 106-131.

Johnston, Trevor, & Schembri, Adam. (2013). Corpus analysis of sign languages. In: Carol A. Chapelle (Ed.), *Encyclopedia of Applied Linguistics* (pp. 479-501). London: Wiley-Blackwell.

Karlsson, Fred. (1984). Structure and Iconicity in Sign Language. In: Filip Loncke, Penny Boyes-Braem, Yvan Lebrun (Eds.). *Recent Research on European Sign Languages* (pp. 149-155). Lisse: Swets & Zeitlinger B.V.

Kendon, Adam. (2014). Semiotic diversity in utterance production and the concept of 'language'. *Phil. Trans. R. Soc. B,* 369, 20130293.

INTRODUCTION

Kyle, Jim, & Allsop, Lorna. (1997). *Sign on Europe: A study of deaf people and sign language in the European Union.* Bristol: University of Bristol, Centre for Deaf Studies.

Kusters, Annelies, De Meulder, Maartje, & O'Brien, Dai. (2017). Innovations in Deaf Studies: Critically mapping the field. In: Annelies Kusters, Maartje De Meulder & Dai O'Brien (Eds.). *Innovations in Deaf Studies: The Role of Deaf Scholars* (pp. 1-53). Oxford: Oxford University Press.

Leeson, Lorraine, Sheikh, Haaris, & Vermeerbergen, Myriam. (2015). The Superhighway or the slow lane? Evaluating challenges in creating new learning spaces for interpreters. In: Suzanne Ehrlich, & Jemina Napier (Eds). *Digital education in interpreter education: innovation, access, and change* (pp. 153-196). (Interpreter Education Series Volume 8). Washington D.C.: Gallaudet University Press.

Le Guen, Olivier. (2012). An exploration in the domain of time: from Yucatec Maya time gestures to Yucatec Maya Sign Language time signs. In: Ulrike Zeshan & Connie de Vos (Eds.), *Endangered Sign Languages in Village Communities: Anthropological and Linguistic Insights* (pp. 209-250). Berlin: Mouton de Gruyter & Ishara Press.

Lepic, Ryan, Börstell, Carl, Belsitzman, Gal, & Sandler, Wendy. (2016). Taking meaning in hand: Iconic motivations in twohanded signs. *Sign Language and Linguistics, 19*(1), 37-81.

Liddell, Scott K. (2000). Blended spaces and deixis in sign language discourse. In: David McNeill (Ed.), *Language and Gesture* (pp. 331-357). Cambridge: Cambridge University Press.

Liddell, Scott K. (2003). *Grammar, Gesture, and Meaning in American Sign Language.* Cambridge: Cambridge University Press.

Liddell, Scott K., & Metzger, Melanie. (1998). Gesture in sign language discourse. *Journal of Pragmatics 30*:6, 657-697.

Lucas, Ceil, Bayley, Robert, & Valli, Clayton. (2001). *Sociolinguistic Variation in American Sign Language.* Washington, D.C.: Gallaudet University Press.

Malmquist, Ann Kristin, & Mosand, Nora Edwardsen. (1996). *Se mitt språk! Språkbok – en innføring i norsk tegnspråk.* Oslo: Døves Forlag AS. [*See my language! Language book – an introduction to Norwegian Sign Language*].

McNeill, David. (1993). "The Circle from Gesture to Sign". In: Marc Marschark & M. Diane Clark (Eds.), *Psychological Perspectives on Deafness* (pp. 153-183). Hillsdale, N.J.: Erlbaum.

Meir, Irit, Sandler, Wendy, Padden, Carol, & Aronoff, Mark. (2010). Chapter 18: Emerging sign languages. In: Marc Marschark & Patricia Elizabeth Spencer (Eds.). *Oxford Handbook of Deaf Studies, Language, and Education. vol. 2.* New York: Oxford University Press.

Metzger, Melanie. (1995). Constructed Dialogue and Constructed Action in American Sign Language. In: Ceil Lucas (Ed.), *Sociolinguistics in Deaf Communities* (pp. 255-271). Washington, D.C.: Gallaudet University Press.

Miller, Chris. (1994). Simultaneous Constructions in Quebec Sign Language. In: Mary Brennan & Graham H. Turner (Eds.), *Word-order Issues in Sign Language. Working Papers* (pp. 89-112). Durham: ISLA.

Moody, Bill. (1983). *Introduction à la Grammaire de la Langue des Signes. Entre les Mains des Sourds.* Vincennes: International Visual Theatre.

Narrog, Heiko, & Heine, Bernd (Eds.) (2011). *The Oxford handbook of grammaticalization.* Oxford: Oxford Univ. Press.

Nilsson, Anna-Lena. (2004). Form and discourse function of the pointing toward the chest in Swedish Sign Language. *Sign Language & Linguistics, 7*(1), 3-30.

Nilsson, Anna-Lena. (2007). The Non-Dominant Hand in a Swedish Sign Language Discourse. In: Myriam Vermeerbergen, Lorraine Leeson, & Onno Crasborn (Eds.). *Simultaneity in Signed Languages: Form and Function* (pp. 163-185). Amsterdam: John Benjamins Publishing Company.

Nilsson, Anna-Lena. (2008). Spatial Strategies in Descriptive Discourse: Use of Signing Space in Swedish Sign Language. In: Lorraine Leeson (Series Ed.), *CDS/SLSCS Monographs* (pp. 88). Dublin, Ireland: Centre for Deaf Studies, University of Dublin, Trinity College, Dublin.

Nyst, Victoria. (2007). *A descriptive analysis of Adamorobe Sign Language (Ghana).* PhD Dissertation. Universiteit van Amsterdam. Utrecht: LOT.

Nyst, Victoria. (2010). Sign languages in West Africa. In: Diane Brentari (Ed.), *Sign Languages* (pp. 405-432).(Cambridge Language Surveys). Cambridge: Cambridge University Press.

Perniss, Pamela. (2007). *Space and Iconicity in German Sign Language.* Doctoral Dissertation. MPI Series 45.

Perniss, Pamela, Pfau, Roland, & Steinbach, Markus. (2007). Can't You See the Difference? Sources of Variation in Sign Language Structure. In: Pamela Perniss, Roland Pfau, & Markus Steinbach (Eds.). *Visible Variation. Comparative Studies on Sign Language Structure* (pp. 1-34). Berlin: Mouton de Gruyter.

Pfau, Roland, Markus Steinbach, & Woll, Bencie (Eds.). (2012). *Sign language: An international handbook.* Boston: Walter de Gruyter.

Pilleux, Mauricio, Cuevas, Hernán, & Avalos, Erica. (1991). *El Lenguaje de Señas. Análisis sintáctico-semántico.* Central de Publicationes, Universidad Austral de Chile.

Prillwitz, Siegmund, & Leven, Regina. (1985). *Skizzen zu einer Grammatik der Deutschen Gebärdensprache.* Hamburg: Forschungsstelle Deutsche Gebärdensprache.

INTRODUCTION

Quinto-Pozos, David. (2007). Can constructed action be considered obligatory? *Lingua, 117*(7), 1159-1354.

Rosenstock, Rachel, & Napier, Jemina (Eds.). (2015). *International Sign. Linguistic, Usage, and Status Issues.* Washington, D.C.: Gallaudet University Press.

Sandler, Wendy. (2003). On the Complementarity of Signed and Spoken Languages. In: Yonata Levy & Jeanette C. Schaeffer (Eds.). *Language Competence across Populations: Toward a Definition of Specific Language Impairment* (pp. 383-409). Mahwah, N.J./London: Erlbaum.

Schembri, Adam. (2001). *Issues in the Analysis of Polycomponential Verbs in Australian Sign Language (Auslan).* Doctoral dissertation, University of Sydney, Sydney.

Schembri, Adam. (2003). Rethinking 'Classifiers' in Signed Languages. In: Karen Emmorey (Ed). *Perspectives on Classifier Constructions in Sign Languages* (pp. 3-34). Mahwah, New Jersey: Lawrence Erlbaum Associates.

Schembri, Adam, Jones, Caroline, & Burnham, Denis. (2005). Comparing Action Gestures and Classifier Verbs of Motion: Evidence from Australian Sign Language, Taiwan Sign Language, and Non-Signers' Gestures Without Speech. *Journal of Deaf Studies and Deaf Education 10*(3), 272-290.

Schermer, Trude, Fortgens, Connie, Harder, Rita, & de Nobel, Esther. (Eds.). (1991). *De Nederlandse Gebarentaal.* Amsterdam: Nederlandse Stichting voor het Dove en Slechthorende Kind/Twello: Van Tricht.

Schwager, Waldemar, & Zeshan, Ulrike. (2008). Word classes in sign languages: Criteria and classification. *Studies in Language 32*(3): 509-545.

Stokoe, William C. Jr. (1960). Sign Language Structure: An outline of the visual communication systems of the American Deaf. *Studies in Linguistics, Occasional Papers, 8.* Buffalo, New York: University of Buffalo.

Supalla, Ted. (1982). *Structure and Acquisition of Verbs of Motion and Location in American Sign Language.* Doctoral dissertation, University of California, San Diego.

Taub, Sarah. (2001). *Language from the Body. Iconicity and Metaphor in American Sign Language.* Cambridge: Cambridge University Press.

Tervoort, Bernard T. (1953). *Structurele analyse van visueel taalgebruik binnen een groep dove kinderen.* [*Structural analysis of visual language use within a group of deaf children*]. Doctoral dissertation, Universiteit van Amsterdam.

Tervoort, Bernard T. (1961). Esoteric Symbolism in the Communication Behavior of Young Deaf Children. *American Annals of the Deaf Vol. 106*(5), 436-480.

Tervoort, Bernard T. (1968). You Me Downtown Movie Fun. *Lingua 21*, 455-465.

Vermeerbergen, Myriam. (1997). *Grammaticale Aspecten van de Vlaams-Belgische Gebarentaal.* Gentbrugge: Cultuur voor Doven.

Vermeerbergen, Myriam (1999). *Grammaticale Aspecten van de Vlaams-Belgische Gebarentaal-videoboek* [*Aspects of the grammar of Flemish-Belgian Sign Language: Signing Book*]. Affligem: Vlaams GebarentaalCentrum.

Vermeerbergen, Myriam. (2006). Past and Current Trends in Sign Language Research. *Language & Communication* 26(2), 168-192.

Vermeerbergen, Myriam, & Demey, Eline. (2007). Sign + Gesture = Speech + Gesture? Comparing Aspects of Simultaneity in Flemish Sign Language to Instances of Concurrent Speech and Gesture. In: Myriam Vermeerbergen, Lorraine Leeson, & Onno Crasborn (Eds.). *Simultaneity in Signed Languages: Form and Function* (pp. 257-282). Amsterdam: John Benjamins.

Vermeerbergen, Myriam, Leeson, Lorraine, & Crasborn, Onno (Eds.). (2007). *Simultaneity in Signed Languages: Form and Function.* Amsterdam: John Benjamins.

Vermeerbergen, Myriam, & Van Herreweghe, Mieke. (2010). Sign Languages and Sign Language Research. In: Jackie Guendouzi, Filip Loncke, & Mandy J. Williams (Eds.). *The Handbook of Psycholinguistic & Cognitive processes: Perspectives in Communication Disorders* (pp. 707-727). London: Taylor & Francis Books.

Vermeerbergen, Myriam, & Leeson, Lorraine. (2011). European Signed Languages – Towards a Typological Snapshot. In: Bernd Kortmann & Johan van der Auwera (Eds.) *The Languages and Linguistics of Europe. A Comprehensive Guide* (pp. 269-287). Berlin: Mouton de Gruyter.

Woll, Bencie. (2003). Modality, universality, and the similarities among sign languages: An historical perspective. In: Anne Baker, Beppie van den Bogaerde & Onno Crasborn (Eds.) *Cross-linguistic Perspectives in Sign Language Research* (pp. 17-27). Hamburg: Signum Verlag.

Zeshan, Ulrike & Pamela Perniss (Eds.). (2008). *Possessive and existential constructions in sign languages.* (Sign Language Typology Series 2). Berlin: De Gruyter Mouton/Nijmegen: Ishara Press.

STRUCTURE OF REFERENCES

Books

1. Monographs

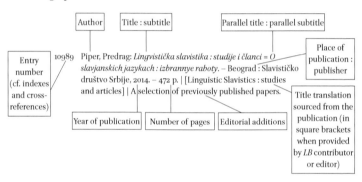

2. Edited volumes

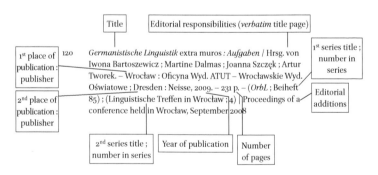

Articles

1. In a periodical

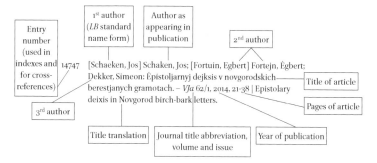

2. In an edited volume

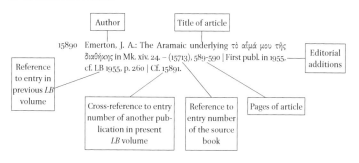

PERIODICALS

This list contains the full titles and abbreviations of periodicals used in this volume. The complete list of periodicals covered in the *Linguistic Bibliography* may be consulted at http://bibliographies.brillonline.com/pages/lb/periodicals.

ARL	Annual review of linguistics. Palo Alto, CA. ISSN: 2333-9691.
B&L	Brain and language : a journal of clinical, experimental, and theoretical research. Oxford. ISSN: 0093-934X.
Bilingualism	Bilingualism : language and cognition. Cambridge. ISSN: 1366-7289. eISSN: 1469-1841.
CILP	Current issues in language planning. London. ISSN: 1466-4208. eISSN: 1747-7506.
Cognition	Cognition : international journal of cognitive science. Amsterdam. ISSN: 0010-0277.
CognL	Cognitive linguistics. Berlin. ISSN: 0936-5907. eISSN: 1613-3641.
ER	Estudis romànics. Barcelona. ISSN: 0211-8572. eISSN: 2013-9500.
Glossa	Glossa : a journal of general linguistics. eISSN: 2397-1835.
GURT	Georgetown University Round Table on Languages and Linguistics. Washington, DC. ISSN: 0196-7207.
HistLing	Rekishi gengogaku = Historical linguistics in Japan. Toyonaka. ISSN: 2187-4859.
IJM	International journal of multilingualism. London. ISSN: 1479-0718. eISSN: 1747-7530.
IJSL	International journal of the sociology of language. Berlin. ISSN: 0165-2516. eISSN: 1613-3668.
JFL	Wàiguóyǔ = Journal of foreign languages. Shànghǎi. ISSN: 1004-5139.
JJLing	Journal of Japanese linguistics. Berlin. ISSN: 0197-3150. eISSN: 2512-1413.
JM&L	Journal of memory & language. Amsterdam. ISSN: 0749-596X. eISSN: 1096-0821.

JPR	Journal of psycholinguistic research. Dordrecht. ISSN: 0090-6905. eISSN: 1573-6555.
JSem	Journal of semantics : an international journal for the interdisciplinary study of the semantics of natural language. Oxford. ISSN: 0167-5133. eISSN: 1477-4593.
LABi	Linguistic approaches to bilingualism. Amsterdam. ISSN: 1879-9264. eISSN: 1879-9272.
LAcq	Language acquisition : a journal of developmental linguistics. Hillsdale, NJ. ISSN: 1048-9223. eISSN: 1532-7817.
Language	Language : journal of the Linguistic Society of America. Baltimore, MD. ISSN: 0097-8507. eISSN: 1535-0665.
LCog	Language and cognition : an interdisciplinary journal of language and cognitive science. Cambridge. ISSN: 1866-9859.
LIA	Language, interaction and acquisition = Langage, interaction et acquisition. Amsterdam. ISSN: 1879-7865. eISSN: 1879-7873.
Linguistics	Linguistics : an interdisciplinary journal of the language sciences. Berlin. ISSN: 0024-3949. eISSN: 1613-396X.
Literator	Literator : journal of literary criticism, comparative linguistics and literary studies = tysdkrif vir besondere en vergelykende taal- en literatuurstudie. Cape Town. ISSN: 0258-2279. eISSN: 2219-8237.
LL	Language learning : a journal of research in language studies. Ann Arbor, MI. ISSN: 0023-8333. eISSN: 1467-9922.
LPLP	Language problems and language planning. Amsterdam. ISSN: 0272-2690. eISSN: 1569-9889.
LPol	Language policy. Dordrecht. ISSN: 1568-4555. eISSN: 1573-1863.
LT	Linguistic typology. Berlin. ISSN: 1430-0532. eISSN: 1613-415X.
ML	The mental lexicon. Amsterdam. ISSN: 1871-1340. eISSN: 1871-1375.
NLLT	Natural language and linguistic theory. Dordrecht. ISSN: 0167-806X. eISSN: 1573-0859.
OpLi	Open linguistics.Warsaw.
PerLinguam	Per linguam : a journal for language learning = tydskrif vir taalaanleer. Stellenbosch. ISSN: 0259-2312. eISSN: 2224-0012.
Polonica	Polonica : rocznik. Polska Akademia Nauk, Instytut Języka Polskiego. Kraków. ISSN: 0137-9712.
RLg	Research in language. Łódź. ISSN: 1731-7533. eISSN: 2083-4616.
SGK	Shakai gengo kagaku = The Japanese journal of language in society. Tōkyō. ISSN: 1344-3909.

PERIODICALS

SKY	SKY : journal of linguistics. Helsinki. ISSN: 1456-8438. eISSN: 1796-297X.
SLLing	Sign language & linguistics. Amsterdam. ISSN: 1387-9316. eISSN: 1569-996X.
SLStud	Sign language studies. Washington, DC. ISSN: 0302-1475. eISSN: 1533-6263.
SPIL	Stellenbosch papers in linguistics. Stellenbosch. ISSN: 1027-3417. eISSN: 2223-9936.
SPILPLUS	Stellenbosch papers in linguistics PLUS. Stellenbosch. ISSN: 1726-541X. eISSN: 2224-3380.
SSLA	Studies in second language acquisition. Cambridge. ISSN: 0272-2631. eISSN: 1470-1545.
Syntax	Syntax : a journal of theoretical, experimental and interdisciplinary research. Oxford. ISSN: 1368-0005. eISSN: 1467-9612.
TGDR	Tōkyō gaikokugo daigaku ronshū. Tōkyō. ISSN: 0493-4342.

ABBREVIATIONS

The following is a list of abbreviations used in the *Bibliography of Sign Languages*. Please note that wherever these abbreviations appear in the titles of publications, they were used so by the authors.

ab.	abstract	fac.	faculty
Acad.	Academy	Fr.	French
Afr.	African	G.	German
art.	article	Hrsg.	Herausgeber, herausgegeben
ass.	association	inst.	institute
biblio.	bibliography	introd.	introduction, introductory
cf.	confer (compare, "see")	LB	Linguistic Bibliography
ch.	chapter	lg.	language
Chin.	Chinese	ling.	linguistic, linguistics
comm.	commentary	n.s.	new series, nouvelle série
conf.	conference	p.	page(s)
cont.	continuation, continued	Pol.	Polish
contr.	contribution(s)	publ.	publication(s), published
coord.	coordinator, coordinated	rev.	review
dir.	direction, directeur, directrice	s.l.	sine loco (no place)
		s.n.	sine nomine (no publisher)
disc.	discussion	Sp.	Spanish
diss.	dissertation	summ.	summary
Du.	Dutch	suppl.	supplement
E.	English	transl.	translation, translated, translator
ed.	edited, editor, edition	univ.	university

BECOME A CONTRIBUTOR TO THE *LINGUISTIC BIBLIOGRAPHY*

The editorial team is looking for specialists who would like to contribute to the *Linguistic Bibliography* by gathering and compiling bibliographical references in their field of expertise.

The *Linguistic Bibliography*, published in annual print volumes and online, is a collection of detailed bibliographical descriptions of linguistic publications on general and language-specific theoretical linguistics. While the bibliography aims to cover all languages of the world, particular attention is given to the inclusion of publications on endangered and lesser-studied languages. Publications in any language are collected, analyzed and annotated (using a state-of-the-art system of subject and language keywords) by an international team of linguists and contributors from all over the world.

If you are interested in joining the *Linguistic Bibliography*, please contact the editors via lb@brill.com.

For more information, visit brill.com/lbcontributor or scan the QR-code below.

General works

3. Conferences, workshops, meetings

1   *Bliskość i oddalenie.Nähe und Ferne.Blízkost a vzdálenost : materiały VI. Międzynarodowej Konferencji Studenckiej Interfaces* we Wrocławiu / Red. Mariusz Dzieweczyński ; Mirjam Jahr ; Kateřina Ondřejová. – Dresden : Neisse, 2009. – 349 p. | Proc. of a conf. held in Wrocław and at Karpacz, 23-30 April 2007 | Ling., 21-144.

2   *Crossing borders in community interpreting : definitions and dilemmas* / Ed. by Carmen Valero-Garcés ; Anne Martin. – Amsterdam : Benjamins, 2008. – xii, 291 p. – (Benjamins translation library ; 76) | Papers from the 2nd International Conference on Public Service Interpreting, Alcalá de Henares, April 2005.

3   *Developments in primate gesture research* / Ed. by Simone Pika ; Katja Liebal. – Amsterdam : Benjamins, 2012. – xiv, 256 p. – (Gesture studies ; 6) | Papers from a workshop "Current developments in non-human primate gesture research", July 2010, Frankfurt am Oder.

4   *Elmélet és empíria a szociolingvisztikában : válogatás a 17. Élőnyelvi Konferencia. – Szeged, 2012. augusztus 30. – szeptember 1. – előadásaiból* / Szerkesztette: Kontra Miklós ; Németh Miklós ; Sinkovics Balázs. – Budapest : Gondolat, 2013. – 562 p. | Theory and empiria in sociolinguistics.

5   *FEL XIX – NOLA : the music of endangered languages : proceedings of the 19th FEL Conference, 7-9 October 2015* / Editors: Nicholas Ostler & Brenda W. Lintinger. – Hungerford : Foundation for Endangered Languages, 2015. – xx, 172 p. | Conference held at Tulane University, New Orleans; hosted by the Tunica-Biloxi Tribe of Louisiana.

6   *Historical linguistics 2011 : selected papers from the 20th International Conference on Historical Linguistics, Osaka, 25-30 July 2011* / Ed. by Ritsuko Kikusawa ; Lawrence A. Reid. – Amsterdam : Benjamins, 2013. – ix, 337 p. – (Current issues in linguistic theory ; 326).

7   *History of linguistics 2008: selected papers from the 11th international*
     conference on the history of the language sciences (ICHOLS XI), Potsdam,
     28 August – 2 September 2008 / Ed. by Gerda Haßler ; with the assis-
     tence of Gesina Volkmann. – Amsterdam : Benjamins, 2011. – xi, 468
     p. – (Amsterdam studies in the theory and history of linguistic science.
     Series 3: studies in the history of the language sciences ; 115).

8   *L'interface langage-cognition = The language-cognition interface : actes*
     du 19e Congres international des linguistes : Geneve, 22-27 juillet 2013
     / Edités par Stephen R. Anderson ; Jacques Moeschler et Fabienne
     Reboul. – Genève : Librairie Droz, 2013. – 436 p. – (Langue et cultures ;
     45).

9   *8th international conference of Greek linguistics = 8ο διεθνές συνέδριο*
     ελληνικής γλωσσολογίας. – Ioannina : Univ. of Ioannina, Dept of
     Linguistics, 2009. – 1292 p. | Ioannina, August 30-September 2, 2007 |
     No eds. given.

10   *Language acquisition and development : proceedings of GALA 2009* /
     Ed. by João Costa ; Ana Castro ; Maria Lobo and Fernanda Pratas. –
     Newcastle : Cambridge scholars, 2010. – xii, 518 p. | Proceedings of the
     biannual conference 'Generative approaches to language acquisition',
     held in Lisbon, 9-11 September 2009.

11   *Language variation : European perspectives V : selected papers from*
     the Seventh International Conference on Language Variation in Europe
     (ICLaVE 7), Trondheim, June 2013 / Ed. by Eivind Torgersen ; Stian
     Hårstad ; Brit Mæhlum ; Unn Røyneland. – Amsterdam : Benjamins,
     2015. – xiii, 240 p. – (Studies in language variation ; 17).

12   *Lessico e lessicologia : atti del XLIV congresso internazionale di studi*
     della Società di Linguistica Italiana (SLI) : Viterbo, 27-29 settembre
     2010 / A cura di Silvana Ferreri. – Roma : Bulzoni, 2012. – xix, 511 p. –
     (Pubblicazioni della Società di Linguistica Italiana ; 56).

13   *Lexical semantics, syntax, and event structure* / Ed. by Malka Rappaport
     Hovav ; Edit Doron ; Ivy Sichel. – New York, NY : Oxford UP, 2010. – xvi,
     401 p. – (Oxford studies in theoretical linguistics ; 27) | Papers from a
     workshop held in honor of Anita Mittwoch, 2006.

14   *I luoghi della traduzione. Le interfacce : atti del XLIII congresso internazi-*
     onale di studi della Società di Linguistica Italiana (SLI), Verona, 24-26
     settembre 2009 / A cura di Giovanna Massariello Merzagora ; Serena Dal
     Maso. – Roma : Bulzoni, 2011. – v, 925 p. – (Pubblicazioni della Società
     di Linguistica Italiana ; 54).

15   *Moving ourselves, moving others : motion and emotion in intersubjec-*
     tivity, consciousness and language / Ed. by Ad Foolen ; Ulrike Lüdtke ;

Timothy P. Racine ; Jordan Zlatev. – Amsterdam : Benjamins, 2012. – viii, 492 p. – (Consciousness & emotion book series ; 6).

16 *Nyelvelmélet és kontaktológia.* 2 / Szerk. Agyagási Klára ; Hegedűs Attila és É. Kiss Katalin. – Piliscsaba ; Budapest : PPKE BTK Elméleti Nyelvészeti Tanszék – Magyar Nyelvészeti Tanszék, 2013. – 257 p. | Language history and language contact. 2.

17 *Proceedings of the thirty sixth annual meeting of the Berkeley Linguistics Society, February 6-7, 2010 : general session; special session: language isolates and orphans; parasession: writing systems and orthography.* – BLS / Editors Nicholas Rolle ; Jeremy Steffman ; John Sylak-Glassman. – Berkeley, CA : Berkeley Linguistics Society, 2016. – vii, 514 p. – (*BLS* ; 36).

18 *Proceedings of the 6th World Congress of African Linguistics, Cologne, 17-21 August 2009* / Ed. by Matthias Brenzinger ; Anne-Maria Fehn. – Köln : Köppe, 2012. – xiv, 658 p.

19 *Proceedings of the xvii euralex international congress : lexicography and linguistic diversity* / Ed. Tinatin Margalitadze, Giorgi Meladze. – Tbilisi : Ivane Javakhishvili Tbilisi State University, 2016. – 918 p. | Conference papers, Tbilisi, 6 – 10 September, 2016.

20 *Proceedings of the 7th world congress of African linguistics, Buea, 17-21 August 2012.* Vol. 1 / Ed. by Gratien G. Atindogbé and Evelyn Fogwe Chibaka. – Cameroon : Langaa RPCIG, 2017. – 542 p. | Not analyzed | Cf. vol. 2, 21.

21 *Proceedings of the 7th world congress of African linguistics, Buea, 17-21 August 2012.* Vol. 2 / Ed. by Gratien G. Atindogbé & Evelyn Fogwe Chibaka. – Cameroon : Langaa RPCIG, 2017. – 542 p. | Not analyzed | Cf. vol. 1, 20.

22 *Procesy rozwojowe współczesnej polszczyzny.* Część I *Najnowsze zjawiska w polszczyźnie : Obrzycko, 23-25 marca 2007* / Pod red. Karoliny Ruty ; Kingi Zalejarz. – Poznań : Poznańskie Studia Polonistyczne, Koło Miłośników Języka przy UAM w Poznaniu, 2009. – 196 p. | Papers presented at a conf. 'Developmental processes of contemporary Polish' held at Obrzycko, 23-25 March 2007.

23 *Prosody and meaning* / Ed. by Gorka Elordieta ; Pilar Prieto. – Berlin : De Gruyter Mouton, 2012. – 383 p. – (Interface explorations ; 25) | Based on the 'Workshop on prosody and meaning' in Barcelona on September 17-18, 2009.

24 *Rich languages from poor inputs* / Ed. by Massimo Piatelli-Palmarini and Robert C. Berwick. – Oxford : Oxford UP, 2013. – xiii, 313 p. | Papers from the workshop 'Rich languages from poor inputs: a workshop in honor of Carol Chomsky', held at MIT in December 2009.

25 *Rightward movement in a comparative perspective* / Ed. by Gert Webelhuth ; Manfred Sailer ; Heike Walker. – Amsterdam : Benjamins, 2013. – viii, 476 p. – (Linguistik aktuell = Linguistics today ; 200) | Papers from a workshop on rightward movement during the annual meeting of the German Linguistic Society (DGfS) in Bamberg in 2008.

26 *Selected papers of the 10th International Conference of Greek Linguistics.100 Διεθνές Συνέδριο Ελληνικής Γλωσσολογίας, Κομοτηνή, 1-4 Σεπτεμβρίου 2011 : πρακτικά : επιλεγμένα κείμενα* / Ed. by = Επιμέλεια Zoe Gavriilidou = Ζωή Γαβριηλίδου ; Angeliki Efthymiou = Αγγελική Ευθυμίου ; Evangelia Thomadaki = Ευαγγελία Θωμαδάκη ; Penelope Kambakis-Vougiouklis = Πηνελόπη Καμπάκη-Βουγιουκλή. – Κομοτηνή : Δημοκρίτειο Πανεπιστήμιο Θράκης, 2012. – 1256 p. | Electronic publ.

27 *Selected proceedings of the 43rd annual conference on African linguistics : linguistic interfaces in African languages* / Ed. by Ọlanikẹ Ọla Orie ; Karen W. Sanders. – Somerville, MA : Cascadilla Proceedings Project, 2013. – vi, 277 p. | Papers from a conference held at Tulane Univ., 15-17 March, 2012 | Also freely available online.

28 *Sign language syntax from a formal perspective : selected papers from the 2012 Warsaw FEAST* / Ed. by Paweł Rutkowski. – Amsterdam : Benjamins, 2013. – p. 119-284. – (*SLLing* ; 16/2) | Special issue.

29 *Signergy* / Ed. by Jac Conradie ; Ronél Johl ; Marthinus Beukes ; Olga Fischer and Christina Ljungberg. – Amsterdam : Benjamins, 2010. – x, 420 p. – (Iconicity in language and literature ; 9) | Selected papers from the Sixth Symposium on Iconicity in Language and Literature, held in Johannesburg, 1-4 April 2007.

30 *Signs of the time : selected papers from TISLR 8* / Ed. by Josep Quer. – Seedorf : Signum, 2008. – xii, 404 p., cd-rom. – (Internationale Arbeiten zur Gebärdensprache und Kommunikation Gehörloser = International studies on sign language and communication of the Deaf ; 51).

31 *Space in language and linguistics : geographical, interactional, and cognitive perspectives* / Ed. by Peter Auer ; Martin Hilpert ; Anja Stukenbrock and Benedikt Szmrecsanyi. – Berlin, Boston : De Gruyter, 2013. – vii, 697 p. – (Linguae & litterae ; 24) | Papers originally presented at a conference series held at the Freiburg Institute for Advanced Studies in the fall of 2009.

32 *Trends in phonetics and phonology : studies from German-speaking Europe* / Adrian Leemann, Marie-José Kolly, Stephan Schmid & Volker Dellwo (eds). – Bern : Lang, 2015. – 406 p. | Selected and revised papers from the 9th *Phonetik & Phonologie* conference, held in Zurich in October 2013.

33   *29. Ulusal dilbilim kurultayı bildirileri, 21-22 Mayıs 2015* / Yayına
      hazırlayanlar: Bekir Savaş ; Doğan Yüksel ; Dilek Fidan ; Bilge Öztürk ;
      Banu İnan Karagül. – İzmit : Kocaeli Üniversitesi Yayınları, 2016. – 179 p.
      | [Papers presented at the 29th conference on Turkish linguistics].

34   *Unity and diversity of languages* / Ed. by Piet van Sterkenburg. –
      Amsterdam : Benjamins, 2008. – xii, 232 p. | Invited papers for the 18th
      International Congress of Linguists (CIL 18), Seoul, 21-26 July 2008.

35   *The Uppsala meeting: proceedings of the 13th International Turkish
      Linguistics Conference* / Ed. by Éva Á. Csató, Birsel Karakoç and
      Astrid Menz. – Wiesbaden : Harrassowitz, 2016. – xv, 293 p. –
      (Turcologica ;110) | Selection of papers presented at the 13th International
      Conference on Turkish Linguistics, held 16-20 August 2006.

36   *Variation, selection, development: probing the evolutionary model of
      language change* / Ed. by Regine Eckardt ; Gerhard Jäger ; Tonjes
      Veenstra. – Berlin : Mouton de Gruyter, 2008. – viii, 408 p. – (Trends
      in linguistics. Studies and monographs ; 197) | Contributions to the 4.
      Blankensee Colloquium on "Language evolution: cognitive and cul-
      tural factors", held in Berlin-Schmöckwitz, 14-16 July 2005.

4. Festschriften and miscellanies

4.1. Festschriften

37   *Social environment and cognition in language development: studies in
      honor of Ayhan Aksu-Koç* / Edited by F. Nihan Ketrez ; Aylin C. Küntay ;
      Şeyda Özçalışkan ; Aslı Özyürek. – Amsterdam : Benjamins, 2017. – xii,
      242 p. – (Trends in language acquisition research ; 21).

38   *Γλώσσης χάριν : τόμος αφιερωμένος από τον Τομέα Γλωσσολογίας στον καθηγητή
      Γεώργιο Μπαμπινιώτη [Georgios **Babiniotis**]* / Επιστημονική επιμέλεια:
      Α. Μόζερ ; Α. Μπακάκου-Ορφανού ; Χ. Χαραλαμπάκης ; Δ. Χειλά-
      Μαρκοπούλου. – Αθήνα : Ελληνικά Γράμματα, 2008. – xxxviii, 704 p. |
      For the sake of language : volume offered by the Linguistics Section to
      Professor Georgios Babiniotis.

39   *Studies in Chinese and Japanese language acquisition: in honor of
      Stephen **Crain*** / Ed. by Mineharu Nakayama ; Yi-ching Su ; Aijun
      Huang. – Amsterdam : Benjamins, 2017. – vi, 286 p. – (Language acqui-
      sition & language disorders ; 60).

40   *Sonic signatures: studies dedicated to John **Harris*** / Ed. by Geoff
      Lindsey ; Andrew Nevins. – Amsterdam : Benjamins, 2017. – x, 322 p. –

(Language faculty and beyond : internal and external variation in linguistics ; 14).

41 *Miscel·lània d'homenatge a Joan **Martí i Castell**.* Vol. 1 *Miscel·lània
    d'homenatge a Joan Martí i Castell I* Vol. 2 *Miscel·lània d'homenatge
    a Joan Martí i Castell II* | Edició a cura de Miquel Àngel Pradilla. –
    Tarragona : Universitat Rovira i Virgili, 2016. – 356; 314 p. – (Universitat
    Rovira i Virgili ; 72) | [Studies in honour of Joan Martí i Castell].

42 *Language typology and historical contingency : in honor of Johanna
    Nichols* | Ed. by Balthasar Bickel ; Lenore A. Grenoble ; David A.
    Peterson ; Alan Timberlake. – Amsterdam : Benjamins, 2013. – viii, 512 p. –
    (Typological studies in language ; 104).

43 *Cum corde et in nova grammatica : estudios ofrecidos a Guillermo **Rojo**.* –
    Santiago de Compostela : Univ. de Santiago de Compostela, 2012. – 927
    p. – (Colección homenaxes) | No eds. given.

44 *Pragmatics and autolexical grammar : in honor of Jerry **Sadock*** | Ed. by
    Etsuyo Yuasa ; Tista Bagchi ; Katharine Beals. – Amsterdam : Benjamins,
    2011. – xxv, 339 p. – (Linguistik aktuell = Linguistics today ; 176).

45 *Różne formy, różne treści : tom ofiarowany Profesorowi Markowi
    Świdzińskiemu* | Red. Mirosław Bańko ; Dorota Kopcińska. – Warszawa :
    Wydział Polonistyki Uniw. Warszawskiego, 2011. – 244 p.

4.2. Miscellanies

46 *Istnieć w kulturze : między teorią a praktyką edukacyjną* | Pod red.
    Małgorzaty Święcickiej ; Danuty Jastrzębskiej-Golonki ; Agnieszki
    Rypel. – Bydgoszcz : Wyd. Uniw. Kazimierza Wielkiego, 2010. – 486 p.

General linguistics and related disciplines

0.1. General

47 *Handbuch Sprache und Wissen* / Hrsg. von Ekkehard Felder und Andreas Gardt. – Berlin : De Gruyter Mouton, 2015 [2014]. – xii, 567 p. – (Handbücher Sprachwissen (HSW) ; 1) | Handbook of language and knowledge.

48 *Naturalness and iconicity in language* / Ed. by Klaas Willems ; Ludovic De Cuypere. – Amsterdam : Benjamins, 2008. – ix, 249 p. – (Iconicity in language and literature ; 7).

0.2. History of linguistics, biographical data, organizations

49 Arık, Engin: Geçmişten geleceğe Türk İşaret Dili araştırmaları. – (615), 7-22 | [History of research related to the Turkish Sign Language].

0.2.1. Western traditions

50 *Encountering Aboriginal languages : studies in the history of Australian linguistics* / Ed. by William B. McGregor. – Canberra : Pacific Linguistics, 2008. – xiv, 526 p. – (Pacific linguistics ; 591).

0.2.1.5. Eighteenth century

51 Raby, Valérie: La phrase expliquée aux sourds-muets : remarques sur la syntaxe chiffrée de l'abbé Sicard. – (7), 277-288 | Roch-Ambroise Sicard (1742-1822) | E. ab.

0.2.1.6. Nineteenth century

52 Ruta, Karolina; [Wrzesniewska, Marta] Wrześniewska-Pietrzak, Marta: Nazwy własne w "Słowniku mimicznym dla głuchoniemych i osób z

nimi styczność mających". – *Onomastica* 59, 2015, 93-106 | Proper names [in] the dictionary titled "Słownik mimiczny dla głuchoniemych i osób z nimi styczność mających" by Józef Hollak and Teofil Jagodziński, 1879 | E. ab.

0.2.1.7.   Twentieth century

53   Hochgesang, Julie A.; Miller, Marvin T.: A celebration of the *Dictionary of American Sign Language on linguistic principles* : fifty years later. – *SLStud* 16/4, 2016, 563-591.

54   Kanda, Kazuyuki: Nihon shuwagaku no ayumi : jibunshiteki shiten kara no essei. – *ShK* 19, 2010, 53-63 | [The advance of Japanese sign linguistics : essay from a personal historical viewpoint] | Special attn. William J. Stokoe (1919-2000).

55   Lerose, Luigi; Berti, Stefania: La lingua dei segni : interpretazione e traduzione, cenni storici. – (14), 229-236.

56   Mori, Sōya; Osonoe, Satoshi: Tokushū taidan : shuwa gengogaku no 50-nen : Nihon no shuwa gengogaku wa sono rekishi kara nani o manabu beki ka. – *ShK* 19, 2010, 11-28 | [Special issue dialogue : fifty years of sign linguistics : what should Japanese sign linguistics learn from its history].

57   *Tokushū : shuwa gengogaku no 50-nen.* – *ShK* | [Ed. by] Nihon shuwa gakkai. – Kyōto. – 66 p. – (*ShK* ; 19) | [Special issue : fifty years of sign linguistics] | Special issue on the occasion of the publication of William C. Stokoe (1919-2000), *Sign Language Structure*, Buffalo, 1960.

0.2.1.8.   Twenty-first century

58   Woodward, James C.; Hoa, Nguyen Thi: Where *Sign language studies* has led us in forty years : opening high school and university education for deaf people in Viet Nam through sign language analysis, teaching, and interpretation. – *SLStud* 13/1, 2012, 19-36 | E. ab.

0.2.4.   Organizations

59   Osonoe, Satoshi: Nihon shuwa gakkai no saisei e mukete. – *ShK* 18, 2009, 11-13 | [Towards the revival of the Japanese Association for Sign Language Studies].

60   Tanaka, Saori: Taiwa no yōyaku toshite no rinri kōryō : Nihon shuwa gakkai rinri kōryō sakutei junbi ni atatte. – *ShK* 18, 2009, 25-30 |

[Statement of ethics : report on the preparations for the compilation of a statement of ethics for the Japanese Association for Sign Language Studies].

0.3. Linguistic theory and methodology

61 [Chen, Deborah] Chen Pichler, Deborah; Hochgesang, Julie A.; Lillo-Martin, Diane C.; Müller de Quadros, Ronice: Conventions for sign and speech transcription of child bimodal bilingual corpora in ELAN. – *LIA* 1/1, 2010, 11-40 | Fr. ab.

62 Courtin, Cyril; Limousin, Fanny; Morgenstern, Aliyah: Évaluer les compétences linguistiques des enfants en langue des signes française : une expérience pionnière. – *LIA* 1/1, 2010, 129-158 | E. ab.

63 Evans, Nicholas; Levinson, Stephen C.: The myth of language universals : language diversity and its importance for cognitive science. 32/5, 2009, 429-448 | Comm. cf. 67 & 64.

64 Harbour, Daniel: Mythomania? : methods and morals from 'The myth of language universals'. – *Lingua* 121/12, 2011, 1820-1830 | Apropos of 63.

65 [Malaia, Evguenia] Malaia, Evie; Wilbur, Ronnie B.: Sign languages : contribution to neurolinguistics from cross-modal research. – *Lingua* 120/12, 2010, 2704-2706 | Cf. 63.

66 *Methods in contemporary linguistics* / Ed. by Andrea Ender ; Adrian Leemann ; Bernhard Wälchli. – Berlin : De Gruyter Mouton, 2012. – xiii, 536 p. – (Trends in linguistics. Studies and monographs ; 247) | In honour of Iwar Werlen.

67 *The myth of language universals.* – *Lingua* / Ed. by Johan Rooryck ; Neil V. Smith ; Anikó Lipták ; Diane Blakemore. – Amsterdam : Elsevier, 2010. – 2651-2758. – (*Lingua* ; 120/12) | Special issue.

68 *The Oxford handbook of linguistic analysis* / Ed. by Bernd Heine ; Heiko Narrog. – Oxford : Oxford UP, 2010. – xxviii, 1016 p. – (Oxford handbooks in linguistics).

69 Primus, Beatrice; Domahs, Ulrike: Laut – Gebärde – Buchstabe. – (47), 125-142 | [Sound – gesture – letter] | G. ab.

70 Sandler, Wendy: The uniformity and diversity of language : evidence from sign language. – *Lingua* 120/12, 2010, 2727-2732 | Cf. 63.

71 Wilcox, Sherman E.; Wilcox, Phyllis P.: The analysis of signed languages. – (68), 739-760.

72 Wilcox, Sherman E.: *Xièěrmàn Wēiěrkǎokèsī rènzhī yǔyánxué yǔ kǒuyǔ hé shǒuyǔ de yīzhì xing shí jiǎng.Ten lectures on cognitive linguistics and the unification of spoken and signed languages* / [Ed. by] Li Fúyìn, Dīng

Yán. – Beijing : Wàiyǔ jiàoxué yǔ yánjiū chūbǎnshè = Foreign language teaching and research press, 2015. – 390 p. – (Shìjiè zhùmíng yǔyán xué jiā xìliè jiǎngzuò = Eminent linguists lectures series).

0.5.   Semiotics

73   *Semblance and signification* / Ed. by Pascal Michelucci ; Olga Fischer ; Christina Ljungberg. – Amsterdam : Benjamins, 2011. – xii, 427. – (Iconicity in language and literature ; 10).

0.5.1.   Non-verbal communication

74   Capirci, Olga; Cristilli, Carla; De Angelis, Valerio; Graziano, Maria: Learning to use gesture in narratives : developmental trends in formal and semantic gesture competence. – (76), 187-200.

75   Günther, Klaus B.; Hennies, Johannes: From pre-symbolic gestures to language : multisensory early intervention in deaf children. – (15), 369-382.

76   *Integrating gestures : the interdisciplinary nature of gesture* / Ed. by Gale Stam ; Mika Ishino. – Amsterdam : Benjamins, 2011. – viii, 372 p. – (Gesture studies ; 4).

77   Kendon, Adam: Kinesic components of multimodal utterances. – *BLS* 35S, 2009 (2010), 36-53.

78   Krifka, Manfred: Functional similarities between bimanual coordination and topic/comment structure. – (36), 307-336 | On signed & spoken lg.

79   Pfau, Roland: A point well taken : on the typology and diachrony of pointing. – (203), 24 p. | Cf. 1191.

80   Szarota, Beata: Sistemi gestuali tecnici e linguaggi dei segni come esempi della comunicazione gestuale alternativa. – *SRP* 36, 2009, 117-125 | E. ab.: Gesture technical systems and sign lgs. as an example of alternative gesture communication.

81   Volterra, Virginia; Capirci, Olga; Caselli, Maria Cristina; Rinaldi, Pasquale; Sparaci, Laura: Developmental evidence for continuity from action to gesture to sign/word. – *LIA* 8/1, 2017, 13-41 | E. & Fr. ab.

82   Vos, Connie de: *Sign-spatiality on Kata Kolok : how a village sign language of Bali inscribes its signing space.* – Nijmegen : Radboud Univ., 2012. – xxi, 496 p. – (MPI series in psycholinguistics ; 72) | PhD dissertation | Electronic publ.

83   Wojda, Piotr: Sztuczne i mieszane języki migowe. – (172), 392-410 |
      Manually coded languages and sign pidgins | Pol. & E. ab.

0.5.2.   Animal communication

84   Leeds, Charles Austin; Jensvold, Mary Lee: The communicative func-
      tions of five signing chimpanzees (*Pan troglodytes*). – *P&C* 21/1, 2013,
      224-247.
85   *Primate communication and human language : vocalisation, ges-
      tures, imitation and deixis in humans and non-humans* / Ed. by Anne
      Vilain ; Jean-Luc Schwartz ; Christian Abry [†] ; Jacques Vauclair. –
      Amsterdam : Benjamins, 2011. – vi, 239 p. – (Advances in interaction
      studies ; 1).

1.   Phonetics and phonology

86   *The segment in phonetics and phonology* / Ed. by Eric Raimy and Charles
      E. Cairns. – Chichester : Wiley-Blackwell, 2015. – x, 348 p.

1.2.   Phonology

87   *The sonority controversy* / Ed. by Steve Parker. – Berlin : De Gruyter
      Mouton, 2012. – xvi, 487 p. – (Phonology and phonetics ; 18).

2.   Grammar, morphosyntax

88   *The expression of possession* / Ed. by William B. McGregor. – Berlin : De
      Gruyter Mouton, 2010. – 435 p. – (The expression of cognitive catego-
      ries ; 2).
89   *On looking into words (and beyond) : structures, relations, analyses* /
      Ed. by Claire Bowern ; Laurence Horn ; Raffaella Zanuttini. – Berlin :
      Language science press, 2017. – xi, 609 p. – (Empirically oriented
      theoretical morphology and syntax ; 3) | A tribute to Stephen R.
      Anderson.

2.1.   Morphology and word-formation

2.1.2.   Derivational morphology

90   *Cross-disciplinary issues in compounding* / Ed. by Sergio Scalise ; Irene
     Vogel. – Amsterdam : Benjamins, 2010. – viii, 382 p. – (Current issues in
     linguistic theory ; 311).

91   Nagano, Akiko: [Rev. art. of] *The Oxford handbook of compounding*,
     ed. by Rochelle Lieber and Pavol Štekauer. – *EngL* 27/2, 2010, 503-515 |
     Cf. 93.

92   Scalise, Sergio; Bisetto, Antonietta: The classification of compounds. –
     (93), 34-53.

93   *The Oxford handbook of compounding* / Ed. by Rochelle Lieber and
     Pavol Štekauer. – Oxford : Oxford UP, 2009. – xx, 691 p.

94   *Word-formation : an international handbook of the languages of Europe*
     / Ed. by Peter O. Müller ; Ingeborg Ohnheiser ; Susan Olsen ; Franz
     Rainer. Vol. 1. – Berlin : De Gruyter Mouton, 2015. – xxii, p. 1-802. –
     (Handbücher zur Sprach- und Kommunikationswissenschaft =
     Handbooks of linguistics and communication science ; 40/1).

95   *Word-formation : an international handbook of the languages of Europe*
     / Ed. by Peter O. Müller ; Ingeborg Ohnheiser ; Susan Olsen ; Franz
     Rainer. Vol. 2. – Berlin : De Gruyter Mouton, 2015. – xii, p. 803-1560. –
     (Handbücher zur Sprach- und Kommunikationswissenschaft =
     Handbooks of linguistics and communication science ; 40/2) | Cf.
     vol. 1, 94.

96   *Word-formation : an international handbook of the languages of
     Europe* / Ed. by Peter O. Müller ; Ingeborg Ohnheiser ; Susan Olsen ;
     Franz Rainer. Vol. 3. – Berlin : De Gruyter Mouton, 2015. – xii, p. 1567-
     2386. – (Handbücher zur Sprach- und Kommunikationswissenschaft =
     Handbooks of linguistics and communication science ; 40/3) | Cf.
     vol. 2, 95.

2.2.   Syntax

97   Aboh, Enoch Oladé; Pfau, Roland: What's a *wh*-word got to do with
     it?. – (101), 91-124.

98   *Challenges to linearization* / Ed. by Theresa Biberauer and Ian
     Roberts. – Berlin : De Gruyter Mouton, 2013. – 379 p. – (Studies in gen-
     erative grammar ; 114).

99   *Correlatives cross-linguistically* / Ed. by Anikó Lipták. – Amsterdam :
     Benjamins, 2009. – vii, 375 p. – (Language faculty and beyond : inter-
     nal and external variation in linguistics ; 1).

100 *Crosslinguistic studies on noun phrase structure and reference* / Ed.
     by Patricia Cabredo Hofherr ; Anne Zribi-Hertz. – Leiden : Brill, 2014
     [2013]. – xii, 401 p. – (Syntax & semantics ; 39).

101 *Mapping the left periphery* / Ed. by Paola Benincà and Nicola Munaro.
     – New York, NY : Oxford UP, 2010. – viii, 339 p. – (The cartography of
     syntactic structures ; 5).

102 Sanfelici, Emanuela: Syntax and morphology : what can compounds
     tell us? : a review article. – *RdL* 23/2, 2011, 351-378 | Cf. 90.

103 *Structuring the argument : multidisciplinary research on verb
     argument structure* / Ed. by Asaf Bachrach ; Isabelle Roy ; Linnaea
     Stockall. – Amsterdam : Benjamins, 2014. – vii, 205 p. – (Language fac-
     ulty and beyond : internal and external variation in linguistics ; 10).

4. Semantics and pragmatics

104 *Imperatives and directive strategies* / Edited by Daniël Van Olmen ;
     Simone Heinold. – Amsterdam : Benjamins, 2017. – vi, 324 p. – (Studies
     in language companion series ; 184).

105 *Pejoration* / Ed. by Rita Finkbeiner ; Jörg Meibauer ; Heike Wiese. –
     Amsterdam : Benjamins, 2016. – vii, 357 p. – (Linguistik aktuell =
     Linguistics today ; 228).

4.1. Semantics

106 *Conceptualizations of time* / Ed. by Barbara Lewandowska-
     Tomaszczyk. – Amsterdam : Benjamins, 2016. – xxi, 325 p. – (Human
     cognitive processing. Cognitive foundations of language structure
     and use ; 52).

107 *Event representation in language and cognition* / Ed. by Jürgen
     Bohnemeyer and Eric W. Pederson. – Cambridge : Cambridge UP, 2011.
     – xiii, 282 p. – (Language, context and cognition ; 11).

108 Herlofsky, William J.: Iconic signs, motivated semantic networks, and
     the nature of conceptualization : what iconic signing spaces can tell
     us about mental spaces. – (29), 301-318.

109 Meir, Irit: Iconicity and metaphor : constraints on metaphorical
     extension of iconic forms. – *Language* 86/4, 2010, 865-896.

4.2. Pragmatics, discourse analysis and text grammar

110   *The conversation frame : forms and functions of fictive interaction* / Ed.
      by Esther Pascual ; Sergeiy Sandler. – Amsterdam : Benjamins, 2016.
      – xi, 384 p. – (Human cognitive processing. Cognitive foundations of
      language structure and use ; 55).

111   *Information structure and agreement* / Ed. by Victoria Camacho
      Taboada ; Ángel L. Jiménez Fernández ; Javier Martín González ;
      Mariano Reyes Tejedor. – Amsterdam : Benjamins, 2013. – vi, 376 p. –
      (Linguistik aktuell = Linguistics today ; 197) | Papers from the 21st
      'Colloquium on generative grammar', held at the Univ. of Seville in
      April 2011.

112   *Quotatives : cross-linguistic and cross-disciplinary perspectives* / Ed. by
      Isabelle Buchstaller ; Ingrid van Alphen. – Amsterdam : Benjamins,
      2012. – xxx, 296 p. – (Converging evidence in language and communi-
      cation research ; 15).

9. Psycholinguistics, language acquisition and neurolinguistics

113   *The shared mind : perspectives on intersubjectivity* / Ed. by Jordan
      Zlatev ; Timothy P. Racine ; Chris Sinha ; Esa Itkonen. – Amsterdam :
      Benjamins, 2008. – xiii, 391 p. – (Converging evidence in language and
      communication research ; 12).

114   *Towards a biolinguistic understanding of grammar : essays on inter-
      faces* / Ed. by Anna Maria Di Sciullo. – Amsterdam : Benjamins, 2012.
      – vi, 368 p. – (Linguistik aktuell = Linguistics today ; 194).

9.1. Origin of language

115   Corballis, Michael C.: The origins of language in manual gestures. –
      (183), 382-386.

116   *The emergence of protolanguage : holophrasis vs compositionality* /
      Ed. by Michael A. Arbib ; Derek Bickerton. – Amsterdam : Benjamins,
      2010. – xi, 181 p. – (Benjamins current topics ; 24) | Papers previously
      published in *Interaction Studies* 9/1 (2008).

117   *The evolutionary emergence of language : evidence an*d *inference* / Ed.
      by Rudolf Botha ; Martin Everaert. – Oxford : Oxford UP, 2013. – xviii,
      334 p. – (Oxford studies in the evolution of language ; 17).

118   Kendon, Adam: Gesture first or speech first in language origins?. –
      (203), 21 p. | Cf. 120.

119   MacNeilage, Peter F.: Lashley's problem of serial order and the evolution of learnable vocal and manual communication. – (85), 139-152.

120   Napoli, Donna Jo; Sutton-Spence, Rachel L.: Sign language humor, human singularities, and the origins of language. – (203), 25 p | Cf. 118.

121   Samuels, Bridget D.: The emergence of phonological forms. – (114), 193-213.

9.2.   Psycholinguistics

122   Anible, Benjamin; Morford, Jill P.: Look both ways before crossing the street : perspectives on the intersection of bimodality and bilingualism. – *Bilingualism* 19/2, 2016, 243-245 | Cf. 349.

123   Dubuisson, Colette; Parisot, Anne-Marie; Vercaingne-Ménard, Astrid: Bilingualism and deafness : correlations between deaf students' ability to use space in Quebec Sign Language and their reading comprehension in French. – (412), 51-71.

124   Engberg-Pedersen, Elisabeth: Cognitive foundations of topic-comment and foreground-background structures : evidence from sign languages, cospeech gesture and homesign. – *CognL* 22/4, 2011, 691-718.

125   Kroll, Judith F.; Bice, Kinsey: Bimodal bilingualism reveals mechanisms of cross-language interaction. – *Bilingualism* 19/2, 2016, 250-252 | Cf. 349.

126   Tang, Gladys: Bimodal bilingualism : factors yet to be explored. – *Bilingualism* 19/2, 2016, 259-260 | Cf. 349.

127   *Viewpoint and the fabric of meaning : form and use of viewpoint tools across languages and modalities* / Ed. by Barbara Dancygier ; Wei-lun Lu ; Arie Verhagen. – Berlin : De Gruyter Mouton, 2016. – viii, 292 p. – (Cognitive linguistics research ; 55).

9.2.1.   Language production

128   Emmorey, Karen D.; Petrich, Jennifer A. F.; Gollan, Tamar H.: Bilingual processing of ASL–English code-blends : the consequences of accessing two lexical representations simultaneously. – *JM&L* 67/1, 2012, 199-210.

129   Liceras, Juana M.: Linguistic theory and the Synthesis Model : beyond feature matching restrictions. – *LABi* 6/6, 2016, 776-781 | Commentary on 159.

130   MacSwan, Jeff: Codeswitching and the timing of Lexical Insertion. – *LABi* 6/6, 2016, 786-791 | Commentary on 159.

131   Pierantozzi, Cristina: Language Synthesis model and the problem of the invisible derivation. – *LABi* 6/6, 2016, 808-811 | Commentary on 159.

132   Putnam, Michael T.; Legendre, Géraldine; Smolensky, Paul: How constrained is language mixing in bi- and uni-modal production? – *LABi* 6/6, 2016, 812-816 | Commentary on 159.

133   Pyers, Jennie E.; Gollan, Tamar H.; Emmorey, Karen D.: Bimodal bilinguals reveal the source of tip-of-the-tongue states. – *Cognition* 112/2, 2009, 323-329.

134   Quer, Josep: One or two derivations in (bimodal) bilinguals : that's the question. – *LABi* 6/6, 2016, 817-821 | Commentary on 159.

135   Schaeffner, Simone; Fibla, Laia; Philipp, Andrea M.: Bimodal language switching : new insights from signing and typing. – *JM&L* 94, 2017, 1-14 | E. ab.

136   Serratrice, Ludovica: Cross-linguistic influence, cross-linguistic priming and the nature of shared syntactic structures. – *LABi* 6/6, 2016, 822-827 | Commentary on 159.

9.2.2.   Language comprehension

137   Morford, Janet; Wilkinson, Erin; Villwock, Agnes; Piñar, Pilar; Kroll, Judith F.: When deaf signers read English : do written words activate their sign translations? – *Cognition* 118/2, 2011, 286-292.

138   Orfanidou, Eleni; Adam, Robert; Morgan, Gary; McQueen, James M.: Recognition of signed and spoken language : different sensory inputs, the same segmentation procedure. – *JM&L* 62/3, 2010, 272-283.

139   Shook, Anthony; Marian, Viorica: Bimodal bilinguals co-activate both languages during spoken comprehension. – *Cognition* 124/3, 2012, 314-324.

9.2.3.   Memory

140   Geraci, Carlo; Gozzi, Marta; Papagno, Costanza; Cecchetto, Carlo: How grammar can cope with limited short-term memory : simultaneity and seriality in sign languages. – *Cognition* 106/2, 2008, 780-804.

141   Hall, Matthew L.; Bavelier, Daphne: Short-term memory stages in sign vs. speech : the source of the serial span discrepancy. – *Cognition* 120/1, 2011, 54-66.

9.3.   Language acquisition

142   *The Cambridge handbook of child language* / Ed. by Edith L. Bavin. –
      Cambridge : Cambridge UP, 2009. – x, 596 p.

143   *Gesture and multimodal development* / Ed. by Jean Marc Colletta ;
      Michèle Guidetti. – Amsterdam : Benjamins, 2012. – xii, 224 p. –
      (Benjamins current topics ; 39) | Collection of art., previously publ. as
      a special issue of *Gesture* 10/2-3, 2010.

144   *The gesture-sign interface in language acquisition.L'interface geste-
      signe dans l'acquisition du langage. – LIA* / Ed. by Aliyah Morgenstern
      and Michèle Guidetti. – Amsterdam : Benjamins, 2017. – p. 1-171. –
      (*LIA* ; 8/1) | Special issue.

145   Smith, Neil V.; Tsimpli, Ianthi-Maria; Morgan, Gary; Woll, Bencie: *The
      signs of a savant : language against the odds*. – Cambridge : Cambridge
      UP, 2011. – xiv, 210 p.

146   *The usage-based study of language learning and multilingualism. –
      GURT* / Lourdes Ortega ; Andrea E. Tyler ; Hae In Park ; Mariko Uno,
      editors. – Washington, DC : Georgetown UP., 2016. – 308 p. – (*GURT*).

9.3.1.   First language acquisition, child language

147   Goldin-Meadow, Susan: Studying the mechanisms of language learn-
      ing by varying the learning environment and the learner. – *LCN* 30/8,
      2015, 899-911.

148   *Variation in the input : studies in the acquisition of word order* / Ed.
      by Merete Anderssen ; Kristine Bentzen ; Marit R. Westergaard. –
      Dordrecht : Springer, 2010. – viii, 276 p. – (Studies in theoretical psy-
      cholinguistics ; 39).

9.3.1.1.   First language acquisition by pre-school children

149   Morgenstern, Aliyah; Caët, Stéphanie; Collombel-Leroy, Marie;
      Limousin, Fanny; Blondel, Marion: From gesture to sign and from ges-
      ture to word : pointing in deaf and hearing children. – (143), 49-78.

150   Seal, Brenda C.; DePaolis, Rory A.: Manual activity and onset of first
      words in babies exposed and not exposed to baby signing. – *SLStud*
      14/4, 2014, 444-465 | E. ab.

9.3.1.2.   First language acquisition by school children

151   Niederberger, Nathalie: Does the knowledge of a natural sign lan-
      guage facilitate deaf children's learning to read and write? : insights
      from French Sign Language and written French data. – (412), 29-50.

9.3.1.3.   Plurilingual language acquisition

152   Pfau, Roland: Switching, blending ... and slipping. – *LABi* 6/6, 2016,
      802-807 | Commentary on 159.
153   Quadros, Ronice Müller de; Lillo-Martin, Diane C.; Pichler, Deborah
      Chen: Sobreposição no desenvolvimento bilíngue bimodal = Code-
      blending in bimodal bilingual development. – *RBLApl* 14/4, 2014, 799-
      834 | E. ab.

9.3.2.   Second language acquisition

154   [Aleksiadou, Artemis] Alexiadou, Artemis: Code-blending and
      Distributed Morphology. – *LABi* 6/6, 2016, 756-759 | Commentary on
      159.
155   Baker, Anne Edith: Incongruent grammar : can the model cope? –
      LABi 6/6, 2016, 760-762 | Commentary on 159.
156   Branchini, Chiara; Donati, Caterina: The extent of language co-
      activation in bimodal bilinguals. – *LABi* 6/6, 2016, 763-767 |
      Commentary on 159.
157   Hell, Janet G. van: Relative language proficiency affects language pro-
      duction in unimodal and bimodal bilinguals. – *LABi* 6/6, 2016, 834-838
      | Commentary on 159.
158   Hulk, Aafke; Bogaerde, Beppie van den: Disentangling internal and
      external factors in bimodal acquisition. – *LABi* 6/6, 2016, 772-775 |
      Commentary on 159.
159   Lillo-Martin, Diane C.; Quadros, Ronice Müller de; Pichler, Deborah
      Chen: The development of bimodal bilingualism : implications for
      linguistic theory. – *LABi* 6/6, 2016, 719-755 | E. ab | Commentaries cf.
      154 ; 155 ; 156 ; 380 ; 158 ; 129 ; 161 ; 130 ; 162 ; 377 ; 152 ; 131 ; 132 ; 134 ; 136 ;
      163 & 157 | Authors' response to commentaries cf. 160.
160   Lillo-Martin, Diane C.; Quadros, Ronice Müller de; Pichler, Deborah
      Chen: Synthesizing commentaries and responses. – *LABi* 6/6, 2016,
      839-848 | Response to commentaries on 159.

161   Lohndal, Terje: The role of underspecification in grammar. – *LABi* 6/6, 2016, 782-785 | Commentary on 159.

162   Morford, Jill P.; Wilcox, Phyllis P.: A tale of two articulators : what bilingualism and multimodality together reveal about language representation and use. – *LABi* 6/6, 2016, 792-798 | Commentary on 159.

163   Steinbach, Markus: Mouthing and demonstrating in bimodal contexts. – *LABi* 6/6, 2016, 828-833 | Commentary on 159.

9.4. Neurolinguistics and language disorders

164   Curtiss, Susan: Revisiting modularity : using language as a window to the mind. – (24), 68-90.

9.4.1. Neurolinguistics

165   Capek, Cheryl M.; Woll, Bencie; MacSweeney, Mairéad; Waters, Dafydd; McGuire, Philip K.; David, Anthony S.; Brammer, Michael J.; Campbell, Ruth: Superior temporal activation as a function of linguistic knowledge : insights from deaf native signers who speechread. – *B&L* 112/2, 2010, 129-134.

166   Courtin, Cyril; Hervé, P.-Y.; Petit, L.; Zago, Laure; Vigneau, M.; Beaucousin, V.; Jobard, G.; Mazoyer, B.; Mellet, E.; Tzourio-Mazoyer, Nathalie: The neural correlates of highly iconic structures and topographic discourse in French Sign Language as observed in six hearing native signers. – *B&L* 114/3, 2010, 180-192.

167   Emmorey, Karen D.; McCullough, Stephen: The bimodal bilingual brain : effects of sign language experience. – *B&L* 109/2-3, 2009, 124-132.

168   Grosvald, Michael; Gutiérrez, Eva; Hafer, Sarah; Corina, David: Dissociating linguistic and non-linguistic gesture processing : electrophysiological evidence from American Sign Language. – *B&L* 121/1, 2012, 12-24.

169   Hu, Zhiguo; Wang, Wenjing; Liú, Hóngyàn; Peng, Danling; Yang, Yanhui; Li, Kuncheng; Zhang, John X.; Ding, Guosheng: Brain activations associated with sign production using word and picture inputs in deaf signers. – *B&L* 116/2, 2011, 64-70.

170   Kovelman, Ioulia; Shalinsky, Mark H.; White, Katherine S.; Schmitt, Shawn N.; Berens, Melody S.; Paymer, Nora; Petitto, Laura Ann: Dual language use in sign-speech bimodal bilinguals : fNIRS brain-imaging evidence. – *B&L* 109/2-3, 2009, 112-123.

171   Valadao, Michelle Nave; Issac, Myriam de Lima; Araujo, Draulio
      Barros de; Santos, Antonio Carlos dos: Visualizando a elaboração da
      linguagem em surdos bilíngues por meio da ressonância magnética
      funcional = Viewing the production of language in bilingual deaf sub-
      jects through functional magnetic resonance imaging. – *RBLApl* 14/4,
      2014, 835-859 | E. ab.

9.4.2. Language disorders

172   *Surdologopedia : teoria i praktyka* / Red. Naukowa Ewa Muzyka-
      Furtak. – Gdańsk : Harmonia Universalis, 2015. – 493 p. |
      [Surdologopedy : theory and practice] | Biblio., 445-487 | Subject
      index, 488-493.

9.4.2.3. Language disorders other than developmental and aphasia

173   Mouvet, Kimberley; Matthijs, Liesbeth; Loots, Gerrit; Taverniers,
      Miriam; Herreweghe, Mieke Van: The language development of a deaf
      child with a cochlear implant. – *LS* 35, 2013, 59-79.

10.   Sociolinguistics and dialectology

10.1.   Sociolinguistics

10.1.2.   Language policy and language planning

174   Miti, Lazarus Musazitame: *Language rights in Southern Africa.* – Cape
      Town : CASAS, 2016. – 165 p. – (CASAS book series ; 118).

10.1.4.   Language loss and maintenance

175   *Endangered languages and languages in danger : issues of documen-
      tation, policy, and language rights* / Edited by Luna Filipović ; Martin
      Pütz. – Amsterdam : Benjamins, 2016. – ix, 413 p. – (Impact. Studies in
      language and society ; 42).
176   *Endangered languages and new technologies* / Ed. by Mari C. Jones. –
      Cambridge : Cambridge UP, 2015. – xv, 211 p.
177   *Keeping languages alive : documentation, pedagogy and revitalization*
      / Ed. by Mari C. Jones and Sarah Ogilvie. – Cambridge : Cambridge UP,
      2013. – xiv, 269 p.

10.2.   Multilingualism, language contact

178   *The handbook of bilingualism and multilingualism* / Ed. by Tej K. Bhatia ; William C. Ritchie. – Chichester : Wiley-Blackwell, 2013. – 964 p. – (Blackwell handbooks in linguistics).

10.2.1.   Multilingualism

179   Baker, Anne Edith; Bogaerde, Beppie van den: Code-mixing in signs and words in input and output from children. – (412), 1-27.

180   *The Cambridge handbook of linguistic code-switching* / Ed. by Barbara E. Bullock ; Almeida Jacqueline Toribio. – Cambridge : Cambridge UP, 2009. – xv, 422 p. – (Cambridge handbooks in linguistics).

10.3.   Linguistic geography

181   *Language, borders and identity* / Ed. by Dominic Watt and Carmen Llamas. – Edinburgh : Edinburgh UP., 2014. – xvii, 268 p., maps.

11.   Comparative linguistics

11.1.   Historical linguistics and language change

182   *New directions in grammaticalization research* / Ed. by Andrew D.M. Smith ; Graeme Trousdale and Richard Waltereit. – Amsterdam : Benjamins, 2015. – xv, 302 p. – (Studies in language companion series ; 166).

183   *The Oxford handbook of language evolution* / Ed. by Maggie Tallerman ; Kathleen R. Gibson. – Oxford : Oxford UP, 2012. – xxv, 763 p. – (Oxford handbooks in linguistics).

11.2.   Linguistic typology, universals of language

184   Cormier, Kearsy; Schembri, Adam C.; Woll, Bencie: Diversity across sign languages and spoken languages : implications for language universals. – *Lingua* 120/12, 2010, 2664-2667 | Cf. 63.

185   *Measuring grammatical complexity* / Ed. by Frederick J. Newmeyer and Laurel B. Preston. – Oxford : Oxford UP, 2014. – xvi, 370 p.

186   *Reciprocals and semantic typology* / Ed. by Nicholas Evans ; Alice R.
       Gaby ; Stephen C. Levinson ; Asifa Majid. – Amsterdam : Benjamins,
       2011. – viii, 349 p. – (Typological studies in language ; 98).

187   Taub, Sarah F.; Galvan, Dennis B.; Piñar, Pilar: The role of gesture in
       crossmodal typological studies. – *CognL* 20/1, 2009, 71-92.

12.   Mathematical and computational linguistics

12.2.   Statistical and quantitative linguistics

12.2.1.   Corpus linguistics

188   *Spoken corpora and linguistic studies* / Ed. by Tommaso Raso ; Heliana
       Mello. – Amsterdam : Benjamins, 2014. – vii, 498 p. – (Studies in
       corpus linguistics ; 61).

Indo-European languages

3. Indo-Iranian

3.1. Indo-Aryan (Indic)

189   *Annual review of South Asian languages and linguistics 2009* / Ed. by Rajendra Singh. – Berlin : De Gruyter Mouton, 2009. – viii, 249 p. – (Trends in linguistics. Studies and monographs ; 222).

11. Romance

11.2. Ibero-Romance

190   *Intonational grammar in Ibero-Romance : approaches across linguistic subfields* / Ed. by Meghan E. Armstrong ; Nicholas Henriksen ; Maria del Mar Vanrell. – Amsterdam : Benjamins, 2016. – xxi, 389 p. – (Issues in Hispanic and Lusophone linguistics ; 6).

11.2.1. Spanish

11.2.1.2. Modern Spanish

191   *La norma lingüística del español* / Estudios coordinados por Edyta Waluch-de la Torre. Vol. 1. – Varsovia : Museo de Historia del Movimiento Popular Polaco, 2011. – 269 p. | Encuentros 2010.

14. Germanic

14.3.   West Germanic

14.3.1.   German

14.3.1.1.   High German

14.3.1.1.4.   New High German

192   *Satztypen des Deutschen* / Hrsg. von Jörg Meibauer; Markus
      Steinbach; Hans Altmann. – Berlin, Boston: De Gruyter, 2013. – x, 941
      p. – (De Gruyter Lexikon).

14.3.2.   Dutch

193   *Language and space: an international handbook of linguistic varia-
      tion.* Vol. 3 *Dutch* / Ed. by Frans Hinskens; Johan Taeldeman. – Berlin:
      De Gruyter Mouton, 2013. – xxi, 937 p., 39 maps. – (Handbücher zur
      Sprach- und Kommunikationswissenschaft = Handbooks of linguis-
      tics and communication science; 30/3).

14.3.5.   English

14.3.5.4.   Modern English

194   Fais, Laurel; Werker, Janet F.; Cass, Bronwyn; Leibowich, Julia; Barbosa,
      Adriano Vilela; Vatikiotis-Bateson, Eric: Here's looking at you, baby:
      what gaze and movement reveal about minimal pair word-object
      association at 14 months. – *LabPhon* 3/1, 2012, 91-124 | Comm. cf. 345.
195   Loehr, Daniel P.: Temporal, structural, and pragmatic synchrony
      between intonation and gesture. – *LabPhon* 3/1, 2012, 71-89 | Comm.
      cf. 345.

15. Balto-Slavic

15.2.   Slavic

15.2.3.   West Slavic

15.2.3.3.   Polish

196   *Pojęcie, słowo, tekst* / Pod red. naukową Renaty Grzegorczykowej ;
      Krystyny Waszakowej. – Warszawa : Wyd. Uniw. Warszawskiego,
      2008. – 289 p.

197   *Wielokodowość komunikacji* / Pod red. Anny Barańskiej. – Łódź :
      Primum Verbum, 2011. – 142 p. – (Poznawać, tworzyć, komunikować).

Eurasiatic languages

1. Uralic and Altaic

1.2. Altaic

1.2.2. Turkic

1.2.2.3. Southwest Turkic (Oghuz)

1.2.2.3.1. Turkish (Osmanli), Balkan dialects, Gagauz

198 *The acquisition of Turkish in childhood* / Ed. by Belma Haznedar ; F. Nihan Ketrez. – Amsterdam : Benjamins, 2016. – viii, 416 p. – (Trends in language acquisition research ; 20).

Languages of Mainland Southeast Asia

1. Sino-Tibetan

1.2.   Sinitic (Chinese)

1.2.2.   Modern Chinese

199   *Space in languages of China : cross-linguistic, synchronic and dia-chronic perspectives* / Dan Xu (ed.). – Dordrecht : Springer, 2008. – vi, 275 p.

Sign languages

200   Arık, Engin: Describing motion events in sign languages. – *PSiCL* 46/4, 2010, 367-390.

201   Buceva, Pavlina; Čakărova, Krasimira: Za njakoi specifiki na žestomimičnija ezik, izpolzvan ot sluchouvredeni lica. – *ESOL* 7/1, 2009, 73-79 | On some specific features of the sign language used by children with hearing disorders.

202   Dammeyer, Jesper: Tegnsprogsforskning : om tegnsprogets bidrag til viden om sprog. – *SSS* 3/2, 2012, 31-46 | Sign language research : on the contribution of sign language to the knowledge of languages | E. ab | Electronic publ.

203   *Deaf around the world : the impact of language* / Ed. by Gaurav Mathur and Donna Jo Napoli. – Oxford : Oxford UP, 2011. – xviii, 398 p.

204   Fischer, Susan D.: Sign languages East and West. – (34), 3-15.

205   *Formational units in sign languages* / Ed. by Rachel Channon ; Harry van der Hulst. – Berlin : De Gruyter Mouton ; Nijmegen : Ishara Press, 2011. – vi, 346 p. – (Sign language typology ; 3) | Not analyzed.

206   Franklin, Amy; Giannakidou, Anastasia; Goldin-Meadow, Susan: Negation, questions, and structure building in a homesign system. – *Cognition* 118/3, 2011, 398-416.

207   *Gebarentaalwetenschap : een inleiding* / Onder red. van Anne E. Baker ; Beppie van den Bogaerde ; Roland Pfau ; Trude Schermer. – Deventer : Van Tricht, 2008. – 328 p.

208   Kendon, Adam: A history of the study of Australian Aboriginal sign languages. – (50), 383-402.

209   Kendon, Adam: *Sign languages of Aboriginal Australia : cultural, semiotic and communicative perspectives.* – Cambridge : Cambridge UP, 2013. – 562 p. | First publ. 1988; cf. 629.

210   Kudła, Marcin: How to sign the other : on attributive ethnonyms in sign languages. – *PFFJ* 2014, 81-92 | Pol. & E. ab.

211   Meurant, Laurence; Sinte, Aurélie; Vermeerbergen, Myriam; Herreweghe, Mieke Van: Sign language research, uses and practices : a Belgian perspective. – (217), 1-14.

212   *Nonmanuals in sign language* / Ed. by Annika Herrmann and Markus Steinbach. – Amsterdam : Benjamins, 2013. – v, 197 p. – (Benjamins current topics ; 53) | Articles previously publ. in *Sign language & linguistics* 14/1, 2011.

213   Petitta, Giulia; Di Renzo, Alessio; Chiari, Isabella; Rossini, Paolo: Sign language representation : new approaches to the study of Italian Sign Language (LIS). – (217), 137-158.

214   Podbevsek, Sabrina: Gebärdensprachen im Internet. – *ZGL* 40/3, 2012, 481-484.

215   Sawicka, Grażyna: Czy język migowy jest językiem? – (46), 371-380 | E. ab.: Is sign language a language?

216   *Sign language : an international handbook edited by Roland Pfau, Markus Steinbach, Bencie Woll* / Ed. by Roland Pfau ; Markus Steinbach ; Bencie Woll. – Berlin : De Gruyter Mouton, 2012. – xii, 1126 p. – (Handbücher zur Sprach- und Kommunikationswissenschaft = Handbooks of linguistics and communication science ; 37) | Not analyzed.

217   *Sign language research, uses and practices : crossing views on theoretical and applied sign language linguistics* / Ed. by Laurence Meurant ; Aurélie Sinte ; Mieke Van Herreweghe ; Myriam Vermeerbergen. – Berlin : De Gruyter Mouton, 2013. – viii, 318 p. – (Sign languages and deaf communities ; 1).

218   *Sign languages* / Ed. by Diane K. Brentari. – Cambridge : Cambridge UP, 2010. – xxi, 691 p. – (Cambridge language surveys).

219   *Sign languages of the world : a comparative handbook* / Ed. by Julie Bakken Jepsen, Goedele De Clerck, Sam Lutalo-Kiingi, William B. McGregor. – Berlin : De Gruyter Mouton ; Preston, UK : Ishara Press, 2015. – xviii, 1000 p. | Not analyzed.

220   Tobin, Yishai: Looking at sign language as a visual and gestural shorthand. – *PSiCL* 44/1, 2008, 103-119.

221   *Where do nouns come from?* / Ed. by John B. Haviland. – Amsterdam : Benjamins, 2015. – v, 140 p. – (Benjamins current topics ; 70) | Contains papers orig. publ. in *Gesture* 13/3, 2013.

222   Wilcox, Sherman E.: Hands and faces : linking human language and non-human primate communication. – (3), 223-239.

234   Takei, Wataru: Gengo o tsukuridasu chikara : hōmusain kenkyū/
       shuwa kenkyū o tsūjite miete kuru mono. – *Energeia* 37, 2012,
       1-15 | E. ab.: The power to give birth to languages: sign language
       research which approaches the relationship between people and
       language.

235   *Tokushū : shuwa kenkyū no rinri. – ShK* / [Ed. by] Nihon shuwa gakkai. –
       Kyōto. – 73 p. – (*ShK* ; 18) | [Special issue : the ethics of sign linguistics]
       | No personal editor mentioned | Special issue.

0.5.   SEMIOTICS

236   Demey, Eline; Herreweghe, Mieke Van; Vermeerbergen, Myriam:
       Iconicity in sign languages. – (48), 189-214.

0.6.   APPLIED LINGUISTICS

237   Eccarius, Petra; Brentari, Diane K.: Handshape coding made easier : a
       theoretically based notation for phonological transcription. – *SLLing*
       11/1, 2008, 69-101.

238   Kamei, Nobutaka: Bunka jinruigakuteki na shiten kara kentōsuru
       shuwa kenkyūsha no soyō. – *ShK* 18, 2009, 19-22 | [Training sign lin-
       guists who do their research from a cultural anthropological point of
       view].

239   Millet, Agnès; Estève, Isabelle: Transcribing and annotating multi-
       modality : how deaf children's productions call into the question the
       analytical tools. – (143), 175-197.

1.   PHONETICS AND PHONOLOGY

240   Hochgesang, Julie A.: Using design principles to consider representa-
       tion of the hand in some notation systems. – *SLStud* 14/4, 2014, 488-
       542 | E. ab.

1.1.   PHONETICS

241   Jantunen, Tommi: Signs and transitions : do they differ phonetically
       and does it matter? – *SLStud* 13/2, 2013, 211-237 | E. ab.

242   Johnson, Robert E.; Liddell, Scott K.: A segmental framework for rep-
       resenting signs phonetically. – *SLStud* 11/3, 2011, 408-463 | E. ab.

243   Johnson, Robert E.; Liddell, Scott K.: Toward a phonetic representa-
      tion of hand configuration : the thumb. – *SLStud* 12/2, 2012, 316-333 |
      E. ab.

244   Sanders, Nathan C.; Napoli, Donna Jo: A cross-linguistic preference
      for torso stability in the lexicon : evidence from 24 sign languages. –
      SLLing 19/2, 2016, 197-231 | E. ab.

245   Sanders, Nathan C.; Napoli, Donna Jo: Reactive effort as a factor that
      shapes sign language lexicons. – *Language* 92/2, 2016, 275-297.

246   Tyrone, Martha E.; Woll, Bencie: Sign phonetics and the motor sys-
      tem : implications from Parkinson's disease. – (30), 43-60.

1.1.1.   ARTICULATORY PHONETICS

247   Eccarius, Petra; Bour, Rebecca; Scheidt, Robert A.: Dataglove measure-
      ment of joint angles in sign language handshapes. – *SLLing* 15/1, 2012,
      39-72.

248   Johnson, Robert E.; Liddell, Scott K.: Toward a phonetic representa-
      tion of hand configuration : the fingers. – *SLStud* 12/1, 2011, 5-45 | E. ab.

1.1.3.   AUDITORY PHONETICS

249   Brentari, Diane K.; González, Carolina; Seidl, Amanda; Wilbur, Ronnie
      B.: Sensitivity to visual prosodic cues in signers and nonsigners. – *L&S*
      54/1, 2011, 49-72.

1.2.   PHONOLOGY

250   Armstrong, David F.; Wilcox, Sherman E.: Gesture and the nature of
      semantic phonology. – *SLStud* 9/4, 2009, 410-416.

251   Channon, Rachel Elizabeth: The symmetry and dominance condi-
      tions reconsidered. – *CLS* 40/1, 2004 (2008), 45-57.

252   Gù, Shēngyùn; Zhāng, Jíshēng: Shǒuyǔ yīnxì yánjiū jí qí lǐlùn
      móxíng. – *JFL* 40/1, 2017, 52-65 | On studies of sign language phonology
      and its theoretical models | Chin. & E. ab.

253   [Malaia, Evguenia] Malaia, Evie; Wilbur, Ronnie B.: What sign lan-
      guages show : neurobiological bases of visual phonology. – (114),
      265-275.

254   Rozelle, Lorna: A cross-linguistic analysis of dependence between
      phonological parameters. – (30), 25-42.

255   Sandler, Wendy: The challenge of sign language phonology. – *ARL* 3, 2017, 43-63 | E. ab.

256   Sandler, Wendy: The phonological organization of sign languages. – *Compass* 6/3, 2012, 162-182.

1.2.1.   SUPRASEGMENTAL PHONOLOGY (PROSODY)

257   Applebaum, Lauren; Coppola, Marie; Goldin-Meadow, Susan: Prosody in a communication system developed without a language model. – *SLLing* 17/2, 2014, 181-212.

258   Hohenberger, Annette: The word in sign language : empirical evidence and theoretical controversies. – *Linguistics* 46/2, 2008, 249-308.

259   Ormel, Ellen; Crasborn, Onno A.: Prosodic correlates of sentences in signed languages : a literature review and suggestions for new types of studies. – *SLStud* 12/2, 2012, 279-315 | E. ab.

2.   GRAMMAR, MORPHOSYNTAX

260   Aronoff, Mark; Padden, Carol A.: Sign language verb agreement and the ontology of morphosyntactic categories. – *TL* 37/3-4, 2011, 143-151 | Comm. on 265.

261   Cormier, Kearsy; Schembri, Adam C.; Woll, Bencie: Pronouns and pointing in sign languages. – *Lingua* 137, 2013, 230-247.

262   Cysouw, Michael: Very atypical agreement indeed. – *TL* 37/3-4, 2011, 153-160 | Comm. on 265.

263   Kuhn, Jeremy: Cross-categorial singular and plural reference in sign language. – *SLLing* 19/1, 2016, 124-131 | Diss. ab. (New York University, 2015).

264   Liddell, Scott K.: Agreement disagreements. – *TL* 37/3-4, 2011, 161-172 | Comm. on 265.

265   Lillo-Martin, Diane C.; Meier, Richard P.: On the linguistic status of 'agreement' in sign languages. – *TL* 37/3-4, 2011, 95-141.

266   Lillo-Martin, Diane C.; Meier, Richard P.: Response to commentaries : gesture, language, and directionality. – *TL* 37/3-4, 2011, 235-246 | Authors' reply to comments on 265.

267   Meier, Richard P.; Lillo-Martin, Diane C.: Response : the apparent reorganization of gesture in the evolution of verb agreement in signed languages. – *TL* 38/1-2, 2012, 153-157 | Response to 747.

268   Nevins, Andrew Ira: Prospects and challenges for a clitic analysis of (A)SL agreement. – *TL* 37/3-4, 2011, 173-187 | Comm. on 265.

269   Pfau, Roland; Quer, Josep: Nonmanuals: their grammatical and pro-
      sodic roles. – (218), 381-402.

270   Quer, Josep: When agreeing to disagree is not enough : further argu-
      ments for the linguistic status of sign language agreement. – *TL* 37/3-
      4, 2011, 189-196 | Comm. on 265.

271   Rathmann, Christian; Mathur, Gaurav: A featural approach to verb
      agreement in signed languages. – *TL* 37/3-4, 2011, 197-208 | Comm. on
      265.

272   Schlenker, Philippe: Iconic features. – *NLS* 22/4, 2014, 299-356 |
      E. ab.

273   Slobin, Dan Isaac: Breaking the molds : signed languages and the
      nature of human language. – *SLStud* 8/2, 2008, 114-130.

274   Steinbach, Markus; Onea, Edgar: A DRT analysis of discourse refer-
      ents and anaphora resolution in sign language. – *JSem* 33/3, 2016, 409-
      448 | DRT = Discourse Representation Theory | E. ab.

275   Steinbach, Markus: What do agreement auxiliaries reveal about the
      grammar of sign language agreement? – *TL* 37/3-4, 2011, 209-221 |
      Comm. on 265.

276   Wilbur, Ronnie B.: Complex predicates involving events, time and
      aspect : is this why sign languages look so similar? – (30), 217-250.

2.1.   MORPHOLOGY AND WORD-FORMATION

277   McNeill, David; Sowa, Claudia: Birth of a morph. – (76), 27-47.

2.1.1.   INFLECTIONAL MORPHOLOGY

278   Borstell, Carl; Lepic, Ryan; Belsitzman, Gal: Articulatory plurality is a
      property of lexical plurals in sign language. – *LInv* 39/2, 2016, 391-407 |
      E. ab.

279   Mathur, Gaurav; Rathmann, Christian: Two types of nonconcatena-
      tive morphology in signed languages. – (203), 35 p. | Cf. 467.

2.1.2.   DERIVATIONAL MORPHOLOGY

280   Meir, Irit; Aronoff, Mark; Sandler, Wendy; Padden, Carol A.: Sign lan-
      guages and compounding. – (90), 301-322.

281   Wilbur, Ronnie B.: Word-formation and sign languages. – (96),
      2225-2251.

282   Cecchetto, Carlo; Geraci, Carlo; [Zucchi, Alessandro] Zucchi, Sandro: Another way to mark syntactic dependencies : the case for right-peripheral specifiers in sign languages. – *Language* 85/2, 2009, 278-320.

283   Costello, Brendan: Sign language serial verb constructions fit into the bigger picture : commentary on Bos (1996). – *SLLing* 19/2, 2016, 252-269 | Comm. on 773.

284   Fischer, Susan D.: Constituent order in sign languages. – *GK* 146, 2014, 1-12 | Jap. ab.

285   Fischer, Susan D.: Crosslinguistic variation in sign language syntax. – *ARL* 3, 2017, 125-147 | E. ab.

286   Franklin, Amy; Giannakidou, Anastasia; Goldin-Meadow, Susan: Negation as structure building in a home sign system. – (44), 261-276.

287   Geraci, Carlo; Quer, Josep: Determining argument structure in sign languages. – (103), 45-60.

288   Kremers, Joost: The syntax of simultaneity. – *Lingua* 122/9, 2012, 979-1003 | On the simultaneity of signs.

289   *A matter of complexity : subordination in sign languages* | Ed. by Roland Pfau ; Markus Steinbach ; Annika Herrmann. – Berlin : De Gruyter Mouton ; Preston, UK : Ishara Press, 2016. – viii, 262 p. – (Sign languages and deaf communities ; 6).

290   Pfau, Roland; Steinbach, Markus: Complex sentences in sign languages : modality – typology – discourse. – (289), 1-35 | E. ab.

291   Sandler, Wendy: Prosody and syntax in sign languages. – *TPhS* 108/3, 2010 (2011), 298-328.

292   Schlenker, Philippe: Sign language and the foundations of anaphora. – *ARL* 3, 2017, 149-177 | E. ab.

293   *Signs and structures : formal approaches to sign language syntax* | Paweł Rutkowski (ed.). – Amsterdam : Benjamins, 2015. – v, 143 p. – (Benjamins current topics ; 71) | Papers orig. publ. in *Sign language & linguistics* 16/2, 2013.

294   Slobin, Dan Isaac: Typology and channel of communication : where do signed languages fit in. – (42), 47-67.

295   Wilbur, Ronnie B.: Internally-headed relative clauses in sign languages. – *Glossa* 2/1, 2017, 25 | E. ab.

296 Wilbur, Ronnie B.: The point of agreement : changing how we think about sign language, gesture, and agreement. – *SLLing* 16/2, 2013, 221-258.

297 Wilcox, Sherman E.; Occhino, Corrine: Constructing signs : *place* as a symbolic structure in signed languages. – *CognL* 27/3, 2016, 371-404.

3.1. LEXICOLOGY

298 Cormier, Kearsy; Quinto-Pozos, David; Sevcikova, Zed; Schembri, Adam C.: Lexicalisation and de-lexicalisation processes in sign languages : comparing depicting constructions and viewpoint gestures. – *L&C* 32/4, 2012, 329-348.

299 Padden, Carol A.; Meir, Irit; Hwang, So-One K.; Lepic, Ryan; Seegers, Sharon; Sampson, Tory: Patterned iconicity in sign language lexicons. – (221), 43-63.

300 *Semantic fields in sign languages : colour, kinship and quantification* / Ed. by Ulrike Zeshan ; Keiko Sagara. – Berlin : De Gruyter Mouton ; Lancaster : Ishara Press, 2016. – vi, 394 p. – (Sign language typology ; 6).

3.2. LEXICOGRAPHY

301 König, Susanne; Konrad, Reiner; Langer, Gabriele: What's in a sign? : theoretical lessons from practical sign language lexicography. – (30), 379-404.

3.2.2. PLURILINGUAL LEXICOGRAPHY

302 [Fourie, Hanelle] Fourie Blair, Hanelle: Buitetekste in 'n elektroniese gebaretaalwoordeboek. – *Lexikos* 24, 2014, 116-154 | E. ab.: Outer texts in an electronic sign language dictionary | E. & Afrikaans ab.

303 [Fourie, Hanelle] Fourie Blair, Hanelle: Woordeboeke en Dowe gebruikers : huidige probleme en die behoefte aan beter oplossings. – *Lexikos* 23, 2013, 113-134 | E. ab.: Dictionaries and Deaf users : current problems and the need for better solutions | E. & Afrikaans ab.

3.4. TERMINOLOGY

304 *Concise lexicon for sign linguistics* / Ed. by Jan Nijen Twilhaar ; Beppie van den Bogaerde. – Amsterdam : Benjamins, 2016. – xi, 230 p.

4.1.   SEMANTICS

305   Arık, Engin: Spatial language : insights from sign and spoken lan-
       guages (Purdue University, West Lafayette, 2009). – *SLLing* 12/1, 2009,
       83-92.
306   Davidson, Kathryn: The nature of the semantic scale : evidence from
       sign language research. – *SLLing* 16/1, 2013, 106-110 | Diss. ab.
307   Erratum to Quer/Steinbach *Ambiguities in sign languages*. – *LRev*
       32/3, 2015, 601 | Cf. 312.
308   Kosecki, Krzysztof: On prototype-related metonymic models in
       signed languages. – *KNf* 61/3, 2014, 511-527.
309   Kosecki, Krzysztof: Western conception of time in signed languages :
       a cognitive linguistic perspective. – (106), 85-101.
310   Lepic, Ryan; Borstell, Carl; Belsitzman, Gal; Sandler, Wendy: Taking
       meaning in hand : iconic motivations in two-handed signs. – *SLLing*
       19/1, 2016, 37-81.
311   Mesch, Johanna; Raanes, Eli; Ferrara, Lindsay: Co-forming real space
       blends in tactile signed language dialogues. – *CognL* 26/2, 2015, 261-
       287 | E. ab.
312   Quer, Josep; Steinbach, Markus: Ambiguities in sign languages. – *LRev*
       32/1, 2015, 143-165 | E. ab | Erratum, cf. 307.
313   Yau, Shun-chiu: The role of visual space in sign language develop-
       ment. – (199), 143-174.
314   [Zucchi, Alessandro] Zucchi, Sandro: Formal semantics of sign
       languages. – *Compass* 6/11, 2012, 719-734.

4.1.1.   LEXICAL SEMANTICS

315   Ghido, Diana: Aspecte ale semanticii lexicale în limbajele mimico-
       gestuale. – *SCL* 60/1, 2009, 63-85 | E. ab.
316   Napoli, Donna Jo: Iconicity chains in sign languages. – (89), 517-545 |
       E. ab.
317   Schlenker, Philippe: Iconic agreement. – *TL* 37/3-4, 2011, 223-234 |
       Comm. on 265.

4.2.   PRAGMATICS, DISCOURSE ANALYSIS AND TEXT GRAMMAR

318   Berge, Sigrid Slettebakk; Raanes, Eli: Coordinating the chain of utter-
       ances : an analysis of communicative flow and turn taking in an

interpreted group dialogue for deaf-blind persons. – *SLStud* 13/3, 2013, 350-371 | E. ab.

319 Bōnō, Mayumi: Shuwa sōgo kōi ni okeru sokkyō shuwa hyōgen : shūfuku no rensa no kanten kara. – *SGK* 19/2, 2017, 59-74 | Improvisational signing in sign language interaction : through the lens of repair sequence.

320 Cartmill, Erica A.; Rissman, Lilia; Novack, Miriam A.; Goldin-Meadow, Susan: The development of iconicity in children's co-speech gesture and homesign. – *LIA* 8/1, 2017, 42-68 | E. & Fr. ab.

321 *Discourse in signed languages* / Cynthia B. Roy, editor. – Washington, D.C. : Gallaudet UP., 2011. – 240 p. – (Sociolinguistics in deaf communities ; 17) | Not analyzed.

322 Jarque, Maria Josep: What about? : fictive question-answer pairs for non-information-seeking functions across signed languages. – (110), 171-192 | E. ab.

323 Mesch, Johanna: Tactile signing with one-handed perception. – *SLStud* 13/2, 2013, 238-263 | E. ab.

324 Sze, Felix Yim Binh; Wei, Monica X.; Wong, Aaron Yiu Leung: Taboos and euphemisms in sex-related signs in Asian sign languages. – *Linguistics* 55/1, 2017, 153-205 | E. ab.

325 Willoughby, Louisa; Manns, Howard; Shimako, Iwasaki; Bartlett, Meredith: Misunderstanding and repair in Tactile Auslan. – *SLStud* 14/4, 2014, 419-443 | E. ab.

5. STYLISTICS

326 Sutton-Spence, Rachel L.; Kaneko, Michiko: *Introducing sign language literature : folklore and creativity.* – London : Palgrave Macmillan, 2016. – 280 p.

7. TRANSLATION

327 Dickinson, Jules; Turner, Graham H.: Sign language interpreters and the role conflict in the workplace. – (2), 231-244.

328 Swabey, Laurie; Gajewski Mickelson, Paula: Role definition : a perspective on forty years of professionalism in sign language interpreting. – (2), 51-80.

7.1   MACHINE TRANSLATION

329   Morrissey, Sara; [Way, Andrew] Way, Andy: Manual labour : tackling machine translation for sign languages. – *MT* 27/1, 2013, 25-64.

330   Stein, Daniel; Schmidt, Christoph; Ney, Hermann: Analysis, preparation, and optimization of statistical sign language machine translation. – *MT* 26/4, 2012, 325-357.

8.   SCRIPT, ORTHOGRAPHY

331   Filhol, Michael: Modèle descriptif des signes pour un traitement automatique des langues des signes [A descriptive model of signs for sign language processing] (Paris 11 University, Limsi. – CNRS, 2008). – *SLLing* 12/1, 2009, 93-100 | Abstract of the author's doctoral diss.

332   Hoffmann-Dilloway, Erika: Writing the smile : language ideologies in, and through, sign language scripts. – *L&C* 31/4, 2011, 345-355.

333   Hulst, Harry van der; Channon, Rachel Elizabeth: Notation systems. – (218), 151-172.

8.1.   ORTHOGRAPHY

334   Hopkins, Jason: Choosing how to write sign language : a sociolinguistic perspective. – *IJSL* 192, 2008, 75-89

9.   PSYCHOLINGUISTICS, LANGUAGE ACQUISITION AND NEUROLINGUISTICS

335   *Assessing literacy in deaf individuals : neurocognitive measurement and predictors* / Donna Morere ; Thomas Allen, editors. – New York : Springer, 2012. – xvi, 268 p.

9.1.   ORIGIN OF LANGUAGE

336   Armstrong, David F.: *Show of hands : a natural history of sign language.* – Washington, D.C. : Gallaudet UP., 2011. – ix, 116 p.

337   Brentari, Diane K.; Goldin-Meadow, Susan: Language emergence. – *ARL* 3, 2017, 363-388 | E. ab.

338   Meir, Irit; Aronoff, Mark; Borstell, Carl; Hwang, So-One K.; İlkbaşaran, Deniz; Kastner, Itamar; Lepic, Ryan; Lifshitz Ben-Basat, Adi; Padden, Carol A.; Sandler, Wendy: The effect of being human and the basis of

grammatical word order : insights from novel communication systems and young sign languages. – *Cognition* 158, 2017, 189-207 | E. ab.

339   Padden, Carol A.: Iconicity in a new sign language. – *CLS* 44/2, 2008 (2010), 213-225.

9.2.   PSYCHOLINGUISTICS

340   Ding, Guosheng: Code-blending and language control in bimodal bilinguals. – *Bilingualism* 19/2, 2016, 246-247 | Cf. 349.

341   Emmorey, Karen; Giezen, Marcel R.; Gollan, Tamar H.: Insights from bimodal bilingualism : reply to commentaries. – *Bilingualism* 19/2, 2016, 261-263 | Cf. 349.

342   Green, David W.: Language control in bimodal bilinguals : multimodality and serial order. – *Bilingualism* 19/2, 2016, 248-249 | Cf. 349.

343   Napoli, Donna Jo; Sutton-Spence, Rachel L.: Limitations on simultaneity in sign language. – *Language* 86/3, 2010, 647-662.

344   Poarch, Gregory J.: What bimodal and unimodal bilinguals can tell us about bilingual language processing. – *Bilingualism* 19/2, 2016, 256-258 | Cf. 349.

345   Wilcox, Sherman E.: Gesture and language, gesture as language, language as gesture : comments on Loehr and Fais et al. – *LabPhon* 3/1, 2012, 125-131 | Comm. on 195 ; 194.

346   Woll, Bencie; MacSweeney, Mairéad: Let's not forget the role of deafness in sign/speech bilingualism. – *Bilingualism* 19/2, 2016, 253-255 | Cf. 349.

9.2.1.   LANGUAGE PRODUCTION

347   Millet, Agnès; Estève, Isabelle: Contacts de langues et multimodalité chez des locuteurs sourds : concepts et outils méthodologiques pour l'analyse. – *JLC* 2/Varia, 2009, 111-131 | On bilingual children using French & French Sign Language.

348   Watkins, Freya; Thompson, Robin L.: The relationship between sign production and sign comprehension : what handedness reveals. – *Cognition* 164, 2017, 144-149 | E. ab.

9.2.2.   LANGUAGE COMPREHENSION

349   Emmorey, Karen; Giezen, Marcel R.; Gollan, Tamar H.: Psycholinguistic, cognitive, and neural implications of bimodal

bilingualism. – *Bilingualism* 19/2, 2016, 223-242 | Commentary cf. 122 ; 340 ; 342 ; 125 ; 346 ; 344 & 126 | Reply to commentaries cf. 341.

350   Fenlon, Jordan; Denmark, Tanya; Campbell, Ruth; Woll, Bencie: Seeing sentence boundaries. – *SLLing* 10/2, 2008, 177-200.

351   Thompson, Robin L.: Iconicity in language processing and acquisition : what signed languages reveal. – *Compass* 5/9, 2011, 603-616.

352   Zeshan, Ulrike: "Making meaning" : communication between sign language users without a shared language. – *CognL* 26/2, 2015, 211-260 | E. ab.

9.2.3.   MEMORY

353   Miozzo, Michele; Petrova, Anna; Fischer-Baum, Simon; Peressotti, Francesca: Serial position encoding of signs. – *Cognition* 154, 2016, 69-80.

354   Spaepen, Elizabet; Coppola, Marie; Flaherty, Molly; Spelke, Elisabeth S.; Goldin-Meadow, Susan: Generating a lexicon without a language model : do words for number count? – *JM&L* 69/4, 2013, 496-505.

9.3.   LANGUAGE ACQUISITION

355   Brentari, Diane K.; Coppola, Marie; Cho, Pyeong Whan; Senghas, Ann: Handshape complexity as a precursor to phonology : variation, emergence, and acquisition. – *LAcq* 24/4, 2017, 283-306 | E. ab.

356   Carrigan, Emily M.; Coppola, Marie: Successful communication does not drive language development : evidence from adult homesign. – *Cognition* 158, 2017, 10-27 | E. ab.

357   Fontana, Sabina: Les langues des signes entre transmission naturelle et artificielle. – *CFS* 67, 2014, 91-114 | E. ab.

358   Hunsicker, Dea; Goldin-Meadow, Susan: Hierarchical structure in a self-created communication system : building nominal constituents in homesign. – *Language* 88/4, 2012, 732-763.

359   Kamada, Mayuko; Matsuzaki, Jō; Sugai, Hiroyuki: Shuwa no kūkanteki hyōgen ni okeru gakushūsha no erā bunseki : "dōshi no itchi" ni cha-kumokushite. – *ShK* 17, 2008, 47-56 | [Error analysis in sign language learners' spatial expressions : focusing on "verb agreement"].

360   Lillo-Martin, Diane C.: Sign language acquisition studies. – (142), 399-415.

361   Morford, Jill P.; Hänel-Faulhaber, Barbara: Homesigners as late learn-
       ers : connecting the dots from delayed acquisition in childhood to
       sign language processing in adulthood. – *Compass* 5/8, 2011, 525-537.

362   Wood, Sandra K.: Acquisition of topicalization in very late learners of
       LIBRAS : degrees of resilience in language. – (203), 24 p. | Cf. 382.

9.3.1.   FIRST LANGUAGE ACQUISITION, CHILD LANGUAGE

363   *Acquiring sign language as a first language.Acquisition d'une langue
       des signes comme langue première.* – *LIA* / Guest ed. by Marie-Anne
       Sallandre ; Marion Blondel. – Amsterdam : Benjamins, 2010. – 158 p. –
       (*LIA* ; 1/1) | Special issue.

364   Evans, Vyvyan: Cooperative intelligence and recipient design as driv-
       ers for language biases in homesign systems. – *LCN* 30/8, 2015, 912-914
       | Cf. 147.

365   Kotowicz, Justyna: Rozwój kompetencji fonologicznych dzieci
       nabywających języki migowe. – *Polonica* 36, 2016, 145-157 |
       Phonological development in children acquiring sign language | E. ab.

366   Magid, Rachel W.; Pyers, Jennie E.: "I use it when I see it" : the role of
       development and experience in deaf and hearing children's under-
       standing of iconic gesture. – *Cognition* 162, 2017, 73-86 | E. ab.

367   *Sign language acquisition* / Ed. by Anne E. Baker ; Bencie Woll. –
       Amsterdam : Benjamins, 2008. – xii, 167 p. – (Benjamins current
       topics ; 14) | Originally publ. as a special issue of *Sign language & lin-
       guistics*, 8/1-2, 2005.

9.3.1.1.   FIRST LANGUAGE ACQUISITION BY PRE-SCHOOL CHILDREN

368   Staden, Annalene van; Badenhorst, Gerhard; Ridge, Elaine: The ben-
       efits of sign language for deaf learners with language challenges. –
       PerLinguam 25/1, 2009, 44-60 | E. ab.

369   Bernardino, Elidéa Lúcia Almeida: The value of interaction in the
       acquisition of a sign language = O valor da interação na aquisição de
       uma língua de sinais. – *RBLApl* 14/4, 2014, 769-798.

370   Lu, Jenny; Jones, Anna; Morgan, Gary: The impact of input quality on
       early sign development in native and non-native language learners. –
       JChL 43/3, 2016, 537-552 | E. ab.

371   [Malaia, Evguenia] Malaia, Evie; Wilbur, Ronnie B.: Early acquisition
       of sign language : what neuroimaging data tell us. – *SLLing* 13/2, 2010,
       183-199.

372   Nader, Julia Maria Vieira; Novaes-Pinto, Rosana do Carmo: Aquisição
       tardia de linguagem e desenvolvimento cognitivo do surdo. – *EstLing*
       40/2, 2011, 929-943 | Late language acquisition and the cognitive devel-
       opment of deaf children.

9.3.1.2.   FIRST LANGUAGE ACQUISITION BY SCHOOL CHILDREN

373   Surian, Luca; Tedoldi, Mariantonia; Siegal, Michael: Sensitivity to con-
       versational maxims in deaf and hearing children. – *JChL* 37/4, 2010,
       929-943.

9.3.1.3.   PLURILINGUAL LANGUAGE ACQUISITION

374   *Deafness and bilingual education.* – *IJBEB* / Ruth Swanwick. – London :
       Routledge, 2010. – 131-271. – (*IJBEB* ; 13/2).
375   Kanto, Laura; Laakso, Marja-Leena; Huttunen, Kerttu: Differentiation
       in language and gesture use during early bilingual development
       of hearing children of Deaf parents. – *Bilingualism* 18/4, 2015,
       769-788.
376   Kanto, Laura; Laakso, Marja-Leena; Huttunen, Kerttu: Use of code-
       mixing by young hearing children of Deaf parents. – *Bilingualism*
       20/5, 2017, 947-964 | E. ab.
377   Morgan, Gary: Trying to make sense of language synthesis. – *LABi* 6/6,
       2016, 799-801 | Commentary on 159.
378   Takkinen, Ritva: Két- és többnyelvűség : jelnyelv és hangzó nyelv
       mint anyanyelvek. – *ÁNyT* 28, 2016, 219-239 | Bi- and multilingual-
       ism : sign language and spoken language as mother tongues | E. and
       Hg. ab.
379   Woll, Bencie: Sign language and spoken language development in
       young children : measuring vocabulary by means of the CDI. – (217),
       15-34.

9.3.2.   SECOND LANGUAGE ACQUISITION

380   Crasborn, Onno A.: What is a sign language? – *LABi* 6/6, 2016, 768-771
       | Commentary on 159.
381   Ortega, Gerardo; Morgan, Gary: Input processing at first exposure to a
       sign language. – *SLR* 31/4, 2015, 443-463 | E. ab.

9.3.2.1.   UNGUIDED SECOND LANGUAGE ACQUISITION

382   Courtin, Cyril: A critical period for the acquisition of a theory of
      mind? : clues from homesigners. – (203), 13 p. | Cf. 362.

9.4.1.   NEUROLINGUISTICS

383   Emmorey, Karen D.: The neurobiology of language : perspectives from
      sign language. – (8), 157-178.
384   Wilcox, Sherman E.; Xavier, André Nogueira: A framework for unify-
      ing spoken language, signed language, and gesture. – *TAL-RLL* 15/1,
      2013, 88-110 | E. & Port. ab.

9.4.2.1.   DISORDERS OF LANGUAGE DEVELOPMENT

385   *Multilingual aspects of signed language communication and disorder*
      / Ed. by: David Quinto-Pozos. – Bristol : Multilingual Matters, 2014. –
      xvi, 264 p. – (Communication disorders across languages).

10.   OCIOLINGUISTICS AND DIALECTOLOGY

386   Edwards, Terra: Sensing the rhythms of everyday life : temporal inte-
      gration and tactile translation in the Seattle deaf-blind community.
      – *LiS* 41/1, 2012, 29-71.
387   *Sign language, sustainable development, and equal opportunities : envi-
      sioning the future for deaf students* / Ed. by Goedele A. M. De Clerck
      and Peter V. Paul. – Washington, D.C. : Gallaudet UP., 2016. – x, 238 p. |
      Not analyzed.

10.1.   SOCIOLINGUISTICS

388   Friedner, Michele: Understanding and not-understanding : what do
      epistemologies and ontologies do in deaf worlds? – *SLStud* 16/2, 2016,
      184-203 | E. ab.
389   Lucas, Ceil: Methodological issues in studying sign language varia-
      tion. – (217), 285-308.
390   Mouvet, Kimberley; Matthijs, Liesbeth; Loots, Gerrit; Puyvelde,
      Martine Van; Herreweghe, Mieke Van: The influence of social dis-
      courses concerning deafness on the interaction between hearing
      mothers and deaf infants : a comparative case study. – (217), 35-62.

391   *Sociolinguistics and deaf communities* / Ed. by Adam C. Schembri and Ceil Lucas. – Cambridge : Cambridge UP, 2015. – ix, 182 p. | Not analyzed.

10.1.1.   LANGUAGE ATTITUDES AND SOCIAL IDENTITY

392   Īzānlū, ʿAlī; Šarīfī, Šahlā: Abzārhā-ye angīxtegī dar nešānehā-ye zabān-e ešāre : barrasī-ye voǧūh-e maʿnāyī-ye dalālat dar yek zabān-e ešāre-ye xānegī. – *PažZab* 2/[1, series no. 3], 1389 [2010-11], 37-56 | Motivation devices in a sign language : the investigation of aspects of signification in a home sign language | Persian ab | E. ab., p. iii.

393   Krausneker, Verena: Ideologies and attitudes toward sign languages : an approximation. – *SLStud* 15/4, 2015, 411-431 | E. ab.

394   Ladd, Paddy; Lane, Harlan: Deaf ethnicity, deafhood, and their relationship. – *SLStud* 13/4, 2013, 565-579.

395   Schmitt, Pierre: Representations of sign language, deaf people, and interpreters in the arts and the media. – *SLStud* 18/1, 2017, 130-147 | E. ab.

10.1.2.   LANGUAGE POLICY AND LANGUAGE PLANNING

396   Adam, Robert: Standardization of sign languages. – *SLStud* 15/4, 2015, 432-445 | E. ab.

397   Batterbury, Sarah C. E.: Language justice for Sign Language Peoples : the UN Convention on the rights of persons with disabilities. – *LPol* 11/3, 2012, 253-272.

398   Berent, Gerald P.: Sign language – spoken language bilingualism and the derivation of bimodally mixed sentences. – (178), 351-374.

399   Eichmann, Hanna: Planning sign languages : promoting hearing hegemony? : conceptualizing sign language standardization. – *CILP* 10/3, 2009, 293-307.

400   Grosjean, François: Bilingualism, biculturalism, and deafness. – *IJBEB* 13/2, 2010, 133-145.

401   Meulder, Maartje De: The legal recognition of sign languages. – *SLStud* 15/4, 2015, 498-506 | E. ab.

402   Meulder, Maartje De; Murray, Joseph J.: Buttering their bread on both sides? : the recognition of sign languages and the aspirations of deaf communities. – *LPLP* 41/2, 2017, 136-158 | E., Du. & Esperanto ab.

403   Meulder, Maartje De: Promotion in times of endangerment : the Sign Language Act in Finland. – *LPol* 16/2, 2017, 189-208 | E. ab.

404   Murray, Joseph J.: Linguistic human rights discourse in deaf commu-
      nity activism. – *SLStud* 15/4, 2015, 379-410 | E. ab.

405   Rayman, Janice: Why doesn't everyone here speak Sign Language? :
      questions of language policy, ideology and economics. – *CILP* 10/3,
      2009, 338-350.

406   Reagan, Timothy G.: *Language policy and planning for Sign
      Languages.* – Washington, D.C. : Gallaudet UP., 2010. – xviii, 252 p. –
      (Sociolinguistics in deaf communities ; 16).

407   [Sibon, Teresa G] Sibón Maccaro, Teresa-G.: La norma lingüística ante
      la codificación en Lengua de Signos Española (LSE). – (191), 261-269 |
      Sp. & E. ab.

408   Snoddon, Kristin: Equity in education : signed language and the
      courts. – *CILP* 10/3, 2009, 255-271.

409   Trovato, Sara: A stronger reason for the right to sign languages. –
      SLStud 13/3, 2013, 401-422 | E. ab.

10.1.4.   LANGUAGE LOSS AND MAINTENANCE

410   Bickford, J. Albert; Lewis, M. Paul; Simons, Gary F.: Rating the vitality
      of sign languages. – *JMMD* 36/5, 2015, 513-527.

10.2.   MULTILINGUALISM, LANGUAGE CONTACT

411   Nyst, Victoria: The significance of African sign languages for African
      linguistics and sign language studies. – (27), 77-81 | Also freely avail-
      able online.

412   *Sign bilingualism : language development, interaction, and mainte-
      nance in sign language contact situations* / Ed. by Carolina Plaza Pust ;
      Esperanza Morales López. – Amsterdam : Benjamins, 2008. – xvi, 389
      p. – (Studies in bilingualism ; 38).

10.2.1.   MULTILINGUALISM

413   Bartha, Csilla; Holecz, Margit; Romanek, Péter Zalán: Bimodális
      kétnyelvűség, nyelvi-szociokulturális változatosság és hozzáférés :
      a JelEsély modell eredményei és távlatai. – *ÁNyT* 28, 2016, 337-370 |
      Bimodal bilingualism, linguistic, socio-cultural diversity and access :
      results and perspectives of the SIGNificant Chance model | E. and
      Hg. ab.

414   Hiddinga, Anja; Crasborn, Onno A.: Signed languages and globaliza-
      tion. – *LiS* 40/4, 2011, 483-505.

415   Kusters, Annelies; Spotti, Massimiliano; Swanwick, Ruth; Tapio, Elina:
      Beyond languages, beyond modalities : transforming the study of
      semiotic repertoires. – *IJM* 14/3, 2017, 219-232 | E. ab.

416   Plaza Pust, Carolina; Morales López, Esperanza: Sign bilingualism :
      language development, interaction, and maintenance in sign lan-
      guage contact situations. – (412), 333-379.

417   Quinto-Pozos, David: Code-switching between sign languages. – (180),
      221-237.

10.2.3. LANGUAGE CONTACT

418   *English in international deaf communication* / Cynthia J. Kellett Bidoli ;
      Elana Ochse. – Bern : Lang, 2008. – 444 p. – (Linguistic insights.
      Studies in language and communication ; 72).

10.3. LINGUISTIC GEOGRAPHY

419   Padden, Carol A.: Sign language geography. – (203), 23 p. | Cf. 421.

11. COMPARATIVE LINGUISTICS

420   Bakker, Peter: Creoles, creole studies and sign languages. – *JPCL* 30/2,
      2015, 357-369.

421   Woodward, James C.: Some observations on research methodology in
      lexicostatistical studies of sign languages. – (203), 21 p. | Cf. 419.

11.1. HISTORICAL LINGUISTICS AND LANGUAGE CHANGE

422   Pfau, Roland: The grammaticalization of headshakes : from head
      movement to negative head. – (182), 9-50.

423   Richardson, Kristina: New evidence for Early Modern Ottoman Arabic
      and Turkish sign systems. – *SLStud* 17/2, 2017, 172-192 | E. ab.

11.2. LINGUISTIC TYPOLOGY, UNIVERSALS OF LANGUAGE

424   Engberg-Pedersen, Elisabeth: Factors that form classifier signs. – (218),
      252-283.

425   Pfau, Roland; Zeshan, Ulrike: Positive signs : how sign language typol-
       ogy benefits deaf communities and linguistic theory. – *LT* 20/3, 2016,
       547-559.

426   Vos, Connie de; Pfau, Roland: Sign language typology : the contribu-
       tion of rural sign languages. – *ARL* 1, 2015, 265-288.

427   Zeshan, Ulrike; Escobedo Delgado, César Ernesto; Dikyuva, Hasan;
       Panda, Sibaji; Vos, Connie de: Cardinal numerals in rural sign lan-
       guages : approaching cross-modal typology. – *LT* 17/3, 2013, 357-396.

12.2.1.   CORPUS LINGUISTICS

428   Fabisiak, Sylwia: Języki migowe a lingwistyka korpusowa. – *JP* 90/4-5,
       2010, 346-353 | Sign languages and corpus linguistics.

12.3.   COMPUTATIONAL LINGUISTICS

429   Sallandre, Marie-Anne; Garcia, Brigitte: Epistemological issues in
       the semiological model for the annotation of sign languages. – (217),
       159-178.

1. American Sign Language

0.3.   LINGUISTIC THEORY AND METHODOLOGY

430   Davidson, Kathryn: Quotation, demonstration, and iconicity. – *L&P*
       38/6, 2015, 447-520 | E. ab.

0.6.   APPLIED LINGUISTICS

431   Geer, Leah C.: Teaching ASL fingerspelling to second-language learn-
       ers : explicit versus implicit phonetic training. – *SLLing* 19/2, 2016, 280-
       284 | Diss. ab.

432   Swaney, Michelle G.; Smith, David Harry: Perceived gaps and the use
       of supplemental materials in postsecondary American Sign Language
       curricula. – *SLStud* 17/3, 2017, 293-321 | E. ab.

1.   PHONETICS AND PHONOLOGY

433   Mirus, Gene R.: Articulatory play among American cuers. – *SLStud*
       14/3, 2014, 382-401 | E. ab.

434   Stewart, Jesse: A quantitative analysis of sign lengthening in American
      Sign Language. – *SLLing* 17/1, 2014, 82-101.

435   Whitworth, Cecily: Features and natural classes in ASL handshapes. –
      SLStud 12/1, 2011, 46-71 | E. ab.

1.1.   PHONETICS

436   Keane, Jonathan; Brentari, Diane K.; Riggle, Jason: Segmentation and
      pinky extension in ASL fingerspelling. – (86), 103-128.

437   Russell, Kevin; Wilkinson, Erin; Janzen, Terry: ASL sign lowering as
      undershoot : a corpus study. – *LabPhon* 2/2, 2011, 403-422 | Comm. cf.
      441.

438   Tyrone, Martha E.; Mauk, Claude E.: Phonetic reduction and variation
      in American Sign Language : a quantitative study of sign lowering. –
      LabPhon 3/2, 2012, 425-453.

439   Tyrone, Martha E.; Mauk, Claude E.: The phonetics of head and body
      movement in the realization of American Sign Language signs. –
      Phonetica 73/2, 2016, 120-140.

440   Tyrone, Martha E.; Mauk, Claude E.: Sign lowering and phonetic
      reduction in American Sign Language. – *JPhon* 38/2, 2010, 317-328.

441   Tyrone, Martha E.: Phonetics of sign location in ASL : comments on
      papers by Russell, Wilkinson, & Janzen and by Grosvald & Corina. –
      LabPhon 3/1, 2012, 61-70 | Comm. on 437 ; 451.

1.1.1.   ARTICULATORY PHONETICS

442   Mauk, Claude E.; Lindblom, Björn; Meier, Richard P.: Undershoot of
      ASL locations in fast signing. – (30), 3-24.

443   Mauk, Claude E.; Tyrone, Martha E.: Location in ASL : insights from
      phonetic variation. – *SLLing* 15/1, 2012, 128-146.

444   Napoli, Donna Jo; Sanders, Nathan C.; Wright, Rebecca A.: On the lin-
      guistic effects of articulatory ease, with a focus on sign languages. –
      Language 90/2, 2014, 424-456.

1.2.   PHONOLOGY

445   Eccarius, Petra; Brentari, Diane K.: Contrast differences across lexical
      substrata : evidence from ASL handshapes. – *CLS* 44/2, 2008 (2010),
      187-201.

446 Eccarius, Petra; Brentari, Diane K.: A formal analysis of phonological contrast and iconicity in sign language handshapes. – *SLLing* 13/2, 2010, 156-181.

447 Geraci, Carlo: Tracing direction to contact : commentary on Wilbur (1985). – *SLLing* 13/2, 2010, 222-227 | Cf. 449.

448 Wilbur, Ronnie B.: Productive reduplication in a fundamentally monosyllabic language. – *LS* 31/2-3, 2009, 325-342.

449 Wilbur, Ronnie B.: The role of contact in the phonology of ASL. – *SLLing* 13/2, 2010, 203-216 | Publ. of a paper presented at the 1985 annual meeting of the Linguistic Society of America in Seattle; with author's preface (201-202) and afterword (217-221) | Cf. 447.

1.2.1. SUPRASEGMENTAL PHONOLOGY (PROSODY)

450 [Chen, Deborah] Chen Pichler, Deborah: Sources of handshape error in first-time signers of ASL. – (203), 29 p. | Cf. 570.

451 Grosvald, Michael; Corina, David P.: Exploring the movement dynamics of manual and oral articulation : evidence from coarticulation. – *LabPhon* 3/1, 2012, 37-60 | Comm. cf. 441.

452 Hall, Matthew L.; Ferreira, Victor S.; Mayberry, Rachel I.: Phonological similarity judgments in ASL : evidence for maturational constraints on phonetic perception in sign. – *SLLing* 15/1, 2012, 104-127.

453 Nicodemus, Brenda: *Prosodic markers and utterance boundaries in American Sign Language interpretation.* – Washington, D.C. : Gallaudet UP., 2009. – 162 p. – (Studies in interpretation ; 5).

454 Nicodemus, Brenda: The use of prosodic markers to indicate utterance boundaries in American Sign Language interpretation. – *SLLing* 11/1, 2008, 113-122 | Ab. of the author's University of New Mexico, Albuquerque, 2007 diss.

455 Wilbur, Ronnie B.: Effects of varying rate of signing on ASL manual signs and nonmanual markers. – *L&S* 52/2-3, 2009, 245-285.

2. GRAMMAR, MORPHOSYNTAX

456 Abner, Natasha: Gettin' together a posse : the primacy of predication in ASL possessives. – *SLLing* 16/2, 2013, 125-156.

457 Abner, Natasha: There once was a verb : the predicative core of possessive and nominalization structures in American Sign Language. – *SLLing* 17/1, 2014, 109-118 | Diss. ab.

458   Fischer, Susan D.; Johnson, Robert E.: Nominal markers in ASL. – *SLLing* 15/2, 2012, 243-250 | Author's preface (p. 241), afterword (p. 251-252), and commentary by Helen Koulidobrova (p. 253-258).

459   Kuhn, Jeremy: ASL loci : variables or features? – *JSem* 33/3, 2016, 449-491 | E. ab.

460   Schlenker, Philippe: Featural variables. – *NLLT* 34/3, 2016, 1067-1088 | E. ab.

461   Thompson, Robin L.; Emmorey, Karen D.; Kluender, Robert E.; Langdon, Clifton: The eyes don't point : understanding language universals through person marking in American Signed Language. – *Lingua* 137, 2013, 219-229.

462   Wilkinson, Erin: Finding frequency effects in the usage of NOT collocations in American Sign Language. – *SLLing* 19/1, 2016, 82-123.

463   Wilkinson, Erin: Morphosyntactic variation in American Sign Language : genre effects on the usage of SELF. – (217), 259-284.

464   [Zucchi, Alessandro] Zucchi, Sandro; Neidle, Carol; Geraci, Carlo; Duffy, Quinn; Cecchetto, Carlo: Functional markers in sign languages. – (218), 197-224.

2.1.   MORPHOLOGY AND WORD-FORMATION

465   Lepic, Ryan: Motivation in morphology : lexical patterns in ASL and English. – *SLLing* 19/2, 2016, 285-291 | Diss. ab.

466   Lepic, Ryan; Padden, Carol A.: A-morphous iconicity. – (89), 489-515 | E. ab.

2.1.1.   INFLECTIONAL MORPHOLOGY

467   Dudis, Paul G.: Some observations on form-meaning correspondences in two types of verbs in ASL. – (203), 16 p. | Cf. 279.

468   Fischer, Susan D.: Verb inflections in American Sign Language and their acquisition by the deaf child. – *SLLing* 12/2, 2009, 187-202.

469   Mathur, Gaurav; Rathmann, Christian: Verb agreement in sign language morphology. – (218), 173-196.

470   Rathmann, Christian; Mathur, Gaurav: Verb agreement as a linguistic innovation in signed languages. – (30), 191-216.

471   Thompson, Robin L.: Eye gaze in American Sign Language : linguistic functions for verbs and pronouns. – *SLLing* 11/1, 2008, 130-135 | Ab. of the author's University of California, San Diego, 2006 diss.

472   Weast, Traci: Questions in American Sign Language : a quantitative
       analysis of raised and lowered eyebrows (The University of Texas at
       Arlington, 2008). – *SLLing* 12/2, 2009, 211-221.

2.1.2.   DERIVATIONAL MORPHOLOGY

473   Abner, Natasha: What you see is what you get.get : surface transpar-
       ency and ambiguity of nominalizing reduplication in American Sign
       Language. – *Syntax* 20/4, 2017, 317-352 | E. ab.
474   Vercellotti, Mary Lou; Mortensen, David R.: A classification of com-
       pounds in American Sign Language : an evaluation of the Bisetto and
       Scalise framework. – *Morphology* 22/4, 2012, 545-579 | Cf. Scalise &
       Bisetto (2009), 92.

2.2.   SYNTAX

475   Davidson, Kathryn; Caponigro, Ivano: Embedding polar interrogative
       clauses in American Sign Language. – (289), 151-181 | E. ab.
476   Gökgöz, Kadir: The nature of object marking in American Sign
       Language : (Purdue University, 2013). – *SLLing* 17/1, 2014, 119-122 | Diss.
       ab.
477   Koulidobrova, Elena: Elide me bare : null arguments in American Sign
       Language. – *NLLT* 35/2, 2017, 397-446 | E. ab.
478   Koulidobrova, Helen: Parallelism revisited : the nature of the null
       argument in ASL as compared to the Romance-style *pro*. – *SLLing*
       15/2, 2012, 259-270.
479   Lillo-Martin, Diane C.; Müller de Quadros, Ronice: Focus construc-
       tions in American Sign Language and Língua de Sinais Brasileira. –
       (30), 161-176.
480   Matsuoka, Kazumi: Dōshi jōshō o mochiita Amerika shuwa kōbun no
       tōgoteki bunseki. – *ShK* 17, 2008, 69-83 | [Syntactic analysis of verb
       raising structures in American Sign Language].
481   Napoli, Donna Jo; Fisher, Jami; Mirus, Gene R.: Bleached taboo-term
       predicates in American Sign Language. – *Lingua* 123, 2013, 148-167 | On
       the syntactic effects of bleaching.
482   Nunes, Jairo; Müller de Quadros, Ronice: Phonetically realized traces
       in American Sign Language and Brazilian Sign Language. – (30),
       177-190.
483   Todd, Peyton: ASL 'topics' revisited. – *SLLing* 11/2, 2008, 184-239.

484   Todd, Peyton: Does ASL really have just two grammatical persons? –
       SLStud 9/2, 2009, 166-210.

485   Weast, Traci: Quantified eyebrow motion : new evidence from
       American Sign Language questions. – *CLS* 44/2, 2008 (2010), 227-242.

486   Wilbur, Ronnie B.: Preference for clause order in complex sentences
       with adverbial clauses in American Sign Language. – (289), 36-64 | E.
       ab.

3.1.   LEXICOLOGY

487   Cormier, Kearsy; Schembri, Adam C.; Tyrone, Martha E.: One hand or
       two? : nativisation of fingerspelling in ASL and BANZSL. – *SLLing* 11/1,
       2008, 3-44.

488   Kowalsky, Jilly; Meier, Richard P.: The sign INSTITUTE and its deriva-
       tives : a family of culturally important ASL signs. – *SLStud* 13/3, 2013,
       291-315 | E. ab.

489   Mirus, Gene R.; Fisher, Jami; Napoli, Donna Jo: Taboo expressions in
       American Sign Language. – *Lingua* 122/9, 2012, 1004-1020.

4.   SEMANTICS AND PRAGMATICS

490   Rankin, Miako: *Form, meaning, and focus in American Sign Language.*
       – Washington, D.C. : Gallaudet UP., 2013. – 148 p. – (Sociolinguistics in
       deaf communities ; 19).

491   Roush, Daniel R.: The expression of the location event-structure met-
       aphor in American Sign Language. – *SLStud* 16/3, 2016, 389-432 | E. ab.

492   Wilkinson, Erin: A functional description of SELF in American Sign
       Language. – *SLStud* 13/4, 2013, 462-490 | E. ab.

4.1.   SEMANTICS

493   Arık, Engin: The expressions of spatial relations during interaction in
       American Sign Language, Croatian Sign Language, and Turkish Sign
       Language. – *PSiCL* 48/2, 2012, 179-201.

494   Caponigro, Ivano; Davidson, Kathryn: Ask, and tell as well: question–
       answer clauses in American Sign Language. – *NLS* 19/4, 2011, 323-371.

495   Cates, Deborah; Gutiérrez, Eva; Hafer, Sarah; Barrett, Ryan; Corina,
       David: Location, location, location. – *SLStud* 13/4, 2013, 433-461 | E. ab.

496   Davidson, Kathryn: 'And' or 'or' : general use coordination in ASL. –
       SemPrag 6, 2013, 4:1-44.

497 Kosecki, Krzysztof: Metaphors and metonymies in American and British Sign Languages : a contrastive cognitive perspective. – *LSil* 35, 2014, 153-172 | E. ab.

498 Kuhn, Jeremy: Dependent indefinites : the view from sign language. – *JSem* 34/3, 2017, 407-446 | E. ab.

499 Schlenker, Philippe: Donkey anaphora : the view from sign language (ASL and LSF). – *L&P* 34/4, 2011, 341-395.

500 Wilbur, Ronnie B.: Nonmanuals, semantic operators, domain marking, and the solution to two outstanding puzzles in ASL. – *SLLing* 14/1, 2011, 148-178.

4.1.1. LEXICAL SEMANTICS

501 [Malaia, Evguenia] Malaia, Evie; Wilbur, Ronnie B.: Kinematic signatures of telic and atelic events in ASL predicates. – *L&S* 55/3, 2012, 407-421.

4.1.2. GRAMMATICAL SEMANTICS

502 Churng, Sarah: Syntax and prosodic consequences in ASL : evidence from multiple WH-questions. – *SLLing* 14/1, 2011, 9-48.

4.2. PRAGMATICS, DISCOURSE ANALYSIS AND TEXT GRAMMAR

503 Beal-Alvarez, Jennifer S.; Trussell, Jessica W.: Depicting verbs and constructed action : necessary narrative components in deaf adults' storybook renditions. – *SLStud* 16/1, 2015, 5-29 | E. ab.

504 Davidson, Kathryn: Scalar implicatures in a signed language. – *SLLing* 17/1, 2014, 1-19.

505 Edwards, Terra: From compensation to integration : effects of the protactile movement on the sublexical structure of Tactile American Sign Language. – *JoP* 69, 2014, 22-41.

506 Frederiksen, Anne Therese; Mayberry, Rachel I.: Who is on First? Investigating the referential hierarchy in simple native ASL narratives. – *Lingua* 180, 2016, 49-68 | E. ab.

507 Hoza, Jack: Five nonmanual modifiers that mitigate requests and rejections in American Sign Language. – *SLStud* 8/3, 2008, 264-288.

508 Janzen, Terry: Composite utterances in a signed language : topic constructions and perspective-taking in ASL. – *CognL* 28/3, 2017, 511-538 | E. ab.

509 Janzen, Terry; Shaffer, Barbara: Intersubjectivity in interpreted inter-
     actions : the interpreter's role in co-constructing meaning. – (113), 333-
     355 | Evidence from American Sign Language.

510 Jones, Stephen: Classifier constructions as procedural referring
     expressions in American Sign Language. – *RLg* 13/4, 2015, 367-391 | E.
     ab.

511 Lieberman, Amy M.: Attention-getting skills of deaf children using
     American Sign Language in a preschool classroom. – *AP* 36/4, 2015,
     855-873.

512 Mulrooney, Kristin Jean: *Extraordinary from the ordinary : personal
     experience narratives in American Sign Language.* – Washington, D.C. :
     Gallaudet UP., 2009. – 184 p. – (Sociolinguistics in deaf communities ;
     15).

513 Parrill, Fey; Stec, Kashmiri; Quinto-Pozos, David; Rimehaug, Sebastian:
     Linguistic, gestural, and cinematographic viewpoint : an analysis of
     ASL and English narrative. – *CognL* 27/3, 2016, 345-369.

514 Quinto-Pozos, David; Mehta, Sarika: Register variation in mimetic
     gestural complements to signed language. – *JoP* 42/3, 2010, 557-584.

515 Quinto-Pozos, David; Reynolds, Wanette: ASL discourse strategies :
     chaining and connecting-explaining across audiences. – *SLStud* 12/2,
     2012, 211-235 | E. ab.

516 Roush, Daniel R.: Language between bodies : a cognitive approach
     to understanding linguistic politeness in American Sign Language. –
     SLStud 11/3, 2011, 329-374 | E. ab.

517 Schlenker, Philippe: Temporal and modal anaphora in sign language
     (ASL). – *NLLT* 31/1, 2013, 207-234.

518 Thumann, Mary: Identifying recurring depiction in ASL presenta-
     tions. – *SLStud* 13/3, 2013, 316-349 | E. ab.

519 Young, Lesa; Morris, Carla D.; Langdon, Clifton: "He said what?!" : con-
     structed dialogue in various interface modes. – *SLStud* 12/3, 2012, 398-
     413 | E. ab.

9. PSYCHOLINGUISTICS, LANGUAGE ACQUISITION AND NEUROLINGUISTICS

520 Morere, Donna A.: Methodological issues associated with sign-based
     neuropsychological assessment. – *SLStud* 14/1, 2013, 8-20 | E. ab.

521 Witkin, Gregory A.; Morere, Donna A.; Geer, Leah C.: Establishment of
     a phonemic clustering system for American Sign Language. – *SLStud*
     14/1, 2013, 21-38 | E. ab.

correlational and multiple regression analyses of the abilities of biliterate deaf adults. – *IJEL* 4/1, 2014, 1-18.

532 Baus, Cristina; Carreiras, Manuel, orcid.org/0000-0001-6726-7613; Emmorey, Karen: When does iconicity in sign language matter? – *LCProc* 28/3, 2013, 261-271.

533 Chamberlain, Charlene; Mayberry, Rachel I.: American Sign Language syntactic and narrative comprehension in skilled and less skilled readers : bilingual and bimodal evidence for the linguistic basis of reading. – *AP* 29/3, 2008, 367-388.

534 Corina, David; Grosvald, Michael; Lachaud, Christian M.: Perceptual invariance or orientation specificity in American Sign Language? : evidence from repetition priming for signs and gestures. – *LCProc* 26/8, 2011, 1102-1135.

535 Corina, David P.; Grosvald, Michael: Exploring perceptual processing of ASL and human actions : effects of inversion and repetition priming. – *Cognition* 122/3, 2012, 330-345.

536 Dupuis, Amanda; Berent, Iris: Signs are symbols : evidence from the Stroop task. – *LCN* 30/10, 2015, 1339-1344.

537 Grosvald, Michael; Corina, David P.: The perceptibility of long-distance coarticulation in speech and sign : a study of English and American Sign Language. – *SLLing* 15/1, 2012, 73-103.

538 Grosvald, Michael; Lachaud, Christian M.; Corina, David: Handshape monitoring : evaluation of linguistic and perceptual factors in the processing of American Sign Language. – *LCProc* 27/1, 2012, 117-141.

539 Grosvald, Michael; Lachaud, Christian M.; Corina, David P.: Influences of linguistic and non-linguistic factors in the processing of American Sign Language : evidence from handshape monitoring. – *BLS* 35S, 2009 (2010), 24-35.

540 Morford, Jill P.; Grieve-Smith, Angus B.; MacFarlane, James; Staley, Joshua; Waters, Gabriel: Effects of language experience on the perception of American Sign Language. – *Cognition* 109/1, 2008, 41-53.

541 Piñar, Pilar; Carlson, Matthew T.; Morford, Jill P.; Dussias, Paola E.: Bilingual deaf readers' use of semantic and syntactic cues in the processing of English relative clauses. – *Bilingualism* 20/5, 2017, 980-998 | E. ab.

542 Weisberg, Jill; McCullough, Stephen; Emmorey, Karen D.: Simultaneous perception of a spoken and a signed language : the brain basis of ASL-English code-blends. – *B&L* 147, 2015, 96-106.

543   Williams, Joshua T.; Newman, Sharlene D.: Connections between fin-
       gerspelling and print : the impact of working memory and temporal
       dynamics on lexical activation. – *SLStud* 16/2, 2016, 157-183 | E. ab.

9.2.3.   MEMORY

544   Hamilton, Harley: Sequential recall and American Sign Language :
       a look at LOT. – *SLStud* 17/2, 2017, 265-276 | E. ab.
545   Morere, Donna A.: The signed verbal learning test : assessing verbal
       memory of deaf signers. – *SLStud* 14/1, 2013, 39-57 | E. ab.

9.3.   LANGUAGE ACQUISITION

546   Brentari, Diane K.; Falk, Joshua; Wolford, George: The acquisition of
       prosody in American Sign Language. – *Language* 91/3, 2015, e144-e168.
547   Novogrodsky, Rama; Henner, Jon; Caldwell-Harris, Catherine L.;
       Hoffmeister, Robert: The development of sensitivity to grammatical
       violations in American Sign Language : native versus nonnative sign-
       ers. – *LL* 67/4, 2017, 791-818 | E. ab.

9.3.1.   FIRST LANGUAGE ACQUISITION, CHILD LANGUAGE

548   Allen, Thomas E.; Enns, Charlotte: A psychometric study of the ASL
       receptive skills test when administered to deaf 3-, 4-, and 5-year-old
       children. – *SLStud* 14/1, 2013, 58-79 | E. ab.
549   Davidson, Kathryn; Mayberry, Rachel I.: Do adults show an effect
       of delayed first language acquisition when calculating scalar
       implicatures? – *LAcq* 22/4, 2015, 329-354.

9.3.1.1.   FIRST LANGUAGE ACQUISITION BY PRE-SCHOOL CHILDREN

550   Allen, Thomas E.: ASL skills, fingerspelling ability, home communica-
       tion context and early alphabetic knowledge of preschool-aged deaf
       children. – *SLStud* 15/3, 2015, 233-265 | E. ab.
551   Bailes, Cynthia Neese; Erting, Carol J.; Erting, Lynne C.; Thumann-
       Prezioso, Carlene: Language and literacy acquisition through parental
       mediation in American Sign Language. – *SLStud* 9/4, 2009, 417-456.
552   [Chen, Deborah] Chen Pichler, Deborah: Using early ASL word order
       to shed light on word order variability in Sign Language. – (148),
       157-177.

553   [Chen, Deborah] Chen Pichler, Deborah: Views on word order in early
       ASL : then and now. – (30), 293-317.

554   Ferjan Ramírez, Naja; Lieberman, Amy M.; Mayberry, Rachel I.: The
       initial stages of first-language acquisition begun in adolescence :
       when late looks early. – *JChL* 40/2, 2013, 391-414.

555   Golos, Debbie: Literacy behaviors of deaf preschoolers during video
       viewing. – *SLStud* 11/1, 2010, 76-99.

556   Hou, Lynn Y-S: Acquiring plurality in directional verbs. – *SLLing* 16/1,
       2013, 31-73.

557   Lillo-Martin, Diane C.; Müller de Quadros, Ronice: Acquisition of the
       syntax-discourse interface : the expression of point of view. – *Lingua*
       121/4, 2011, 623-636 | Evidence from American Sign Language and
       Brazilian Sign Language.

9.3.1.2.   FIRST LANGUAGE ACQUISITION BY SCHOOL CHILDREN

558   Novogrodsky, Rama; Fish, Sarah; Hoffmeister, Robert: The acquisi-
       tion of synonyms in American Sign Language (ASL) : toward a further
       understanding of the components of ASL vocabulary knowledge. –
       SLStud 14/2, 2014, 225-249 | E. ab.

9.3.1.3.   PLURILINGUAL LANGUAGE ACQUISITION

559   Giezen, Marcel R.; Emmorey, Karen: Evidence for a bimodal bilin-
       gual disadvantage in letter fluency. – *Bilingualism* 20/1, 2017, 42-48 |
       E. ab.

560   Koulidobrova, Elena V.: Language interaction effects in bimodal bilin-
       gualism : argument omission in the languages of hearing ASL-English
       bilinguals. – *LABi* 7/5, 2017, 583-613 | E. ab.

561   Lillo-Martin, Diane C.; Müller de Quadros, Ronice; Koulidobrova,
       Helen; [Chen, Deborah] Chen Pichler, Deborah: Bimodal bilingual
       cross-language influence in unexpected domains. – (10), 264-275 | On
       the development of a sign lg. and a spoken lg. in two pairs: American
       Sign Language & American English, and Brazilian Sign Language &
       Brazilian Portuguese.

562   Mann, Wolfgang; Shèng, Lì; Morgan, Gary: Lexical-semantic organi-
       zation in bilingually developing deaf children with ASL-dominant
       language exposure : evidence from a repeated meaning association
       task. – *LL* 66/4, 2016, 872-899 | E. ab.

9.3.2.   SECOND LANGUAGE ACQUISITION

563   Hilger, Allison I.; Loucks, Torrey M. J.; Quinto-Pozos, David; Dye,
       Matthew W. G.: Second language acquisition across modalities :
       production variability in adult L2 learners of American Sign
       Language. – *SLR* 31/3, 2015, 375-388 | E. ab.

564   Morford, Jill P.; Kroll, Judith F.; Piñar, Pilar; Wilkinson, Erin: Bilingual
       word recognition in deaf and hearing signers : effects of proficiency
       and language dominance on cross-language activation. – *SLR* 30/2,
       2014, 251-271 | E. ab.

565   Morford, Jill P.; [Occhino, Corrine] Occhino-Kehoe, Corrine; Piñar,
       Pilar; Wilkinson, Erin; Kroll, Judith F.: The time course of cross-
       language activation in deaf ASL-English bilinguals. – *Bilingualism*
       20/2, 2017, 337-350 | E. ab.

566   Williams, Joshua T.; Newman, Sharlene D.: Interlanguage dynamics
       and lexical networks in nonnative L2 signers of ASL : cross-modal
       rhyme priming. – *Bilingualism* 19/3, 2016, 453-470.

567   Williams, Joshua T.; Newman, Sharlene D.: Modality-independent
       effect of phonological neighborhood structure on initial L2 sign lan-
       guage learning. – *RLg* 13/2, 2015, 198-212 | E. ab.

568   Williams, Joshua T.; Newman, Sharlene D.: Spoken language activa-
       tion alters subsequent sign language activation in L2 learners of
       American Sign Language. – *JPR* 46/1, 2017, 211-225 | E. ab.

569   Wolbers, Kimberly A.; Bowers, Lisa M.; Dostal, Hannah M.; Graham,
       Shannon C.: Deaf writers' application of American Sign Language
       knowledge to English. – *IJBEB* 17/4, 2014, 410-428.

9.3.2.1.   UNGUIDED SECOND LANGUAGE ACQUISITION

570   Rosen, Russel S.: Modality and language in the second language acqui-
       sition of American Sign Language. – (203), 6 p. | Cf. 450.

9.3.2.2.   GUIDED SECOND LANGUAGE ACQUISITION

571   Rosen, Russel S.: American Sign Language curricula : a review. –
       SLStud 10/3, 2010, 348-381.

572   Williams, Joshua T.; Darcy, Isabelle; Newman, Sharlene D.: The benefi-
       cial role of L1 spoken language skills on initial L2 sign language learn-
       ing : cognitive and linguistic predictors of M2L2 acquisition. – *SSLA*
       39/4, 2017, 833-850 | E. ab.

573   Williams, Joshua T.; Newman, Sharlene D.: Phonological substitution
       errors in L2 ASL sentence processing by hearing M2L2 learners. – *SLR*
       32/3, 2016, 347-366 | E. ab.

9.4.1.   NEUROLINGUISTICS

574   Emmorey, Karen; McCullough, Stephen; Weisberg, Jill: Neural corre-
       lates of fingerspelling, text, and sign processing in deaf American Sign
       Language–English bilinguals. – *LCN* 30/6, 2015, 749-767.

575   Emmorey, Karen; Mehta, Sonya; McCullough, Stephen; Grabowski,
       Thomas J.: The neural circuits recruited for the production of signs
       and fingerspelled words. – *B&L* 160, 2016, 30-41 | E. ab.

576   Malaia, Evguenia; Wilbur, Ronnie B.; Talavage, Thomas: Experimental
       evidence of event structure effects on American Sign Language
       predicate production and neural processing. – *CLS* 44/2, 2008 (2010),
       203-211.

577   Meade, Gabriela; Midgley, Katherine J.; [Sevcikova, Zed] Sevcikova-
       Sehyr, Zed; Holcomb, Phillip J.; Emmorey, Karen: Implicit co-
       activation of American Sign Language in deaf readers : an ERP
       study. – *B&L* 170, 2017, 50-61 | E. ab.

9.4.2.3.   LANGUAGE DISORDERS OTHER THAN DEVELOPMENTAL AND APHASIA

578   Shield, Aaron: The signing of deaf children with autism : lexical pho-
       nology and perspective-taking in the visual-spatial modality (The
       University of Texas at Austin, 2010). – *SLLing* 14/1, 2011, 207-212.

10.1.   SOCIOLINGUISTICS

579   Hill, Joseph: The importance of the sociohistorical context in
       sociolinguistics : the case of Black ASL. – *SLStud* 18/1, 2017, 41-57 |
       E. ab.

580   Lucas, Ceil; Bayley, Robert: Variation in American Sign Language. –
       (218), 451-475.

581   Nicodemus, Brenda; Swabey, Laurie; Leeson, Lorraine; Napier, Jemina;
       Petitta, Giulia; Taylor, Marty M.: A cross-linguistic analysis of finger-
       spelling production by sign language interpreters. – *SLStud* 17/2, 2017,
       143-171 | E. ab.

582   Palmer, Jeffrey Levi; Reynolds, Wanette; Minor, Rebecca: "You want
       what on your PIZZA!?" : videophone and video-relay service as

potential influences on the lexical standardization of American Sign Language. – *SLStud* 12/3, 2012, 371-397 | E. ab.

583 Schneider, Erin; Kozak, L. Viola; Santiago, Roberto; Stephen, Anika: The effects of electronic communication on American Sign Language. – *SLStud* 12/3, 2012, 347-370 | E. ab.

584 Snoddon, Kristin: *American Sign Language and early literacy : a model parent-child program.* – Washington, D.C. : Gallaudet UP., 2012. – xi, 142 p.

10.1.1.   LANGUAGE ATTITUDES AND SOCIAL IDENTITY

585 Bauman, H-Dirksen L.: American Sign Language music videos : language preservation or denigration?. – (5), 110-116.

586 Blau, Shane: Indexing gay identities in American Sign Language. – *SLStud* 18/1, 2017, 5-40 | E. ab.

587 Hill, Joseph: *Language attitudes in the American deaf community.* – Washington, D.C. : Gallaudet UP., 2012. – xiv, 194 p. – (Sociolinguistics in deaf communities ; 18).

588 McDermid, Campbell: The dialectic of second-language learning : on becoming an ASL-English interpreter. – *SLStud* 17/4, 2017, 450-480 | E. ab.

589 Parks, Elizabeth S.: Constructing national and international deaf identity : perceived use of American Sign Language. – (181), 206-217.

590 Reagan, Timothy G.: Ideological barriers to American Sign Language : unpacking linguistic resistance. – *SLStud* 11/4, 2011, 606-636 | E. ab.

10.1.2.   LANGUAGE POLICY AND LANGUAGE PLANNING

591 Cooper, Sheryl B.; Reisman, Joel I.; Watson, Douglas: Sign language program structure and content in institutions of higher education in the United States, 1994-2004. – *SLStud* 11/3, 2011, 298-328.

10.2.1.   MULTILINGUALISM

592 Bishop, Michele: Happen can't hear : an analysis of code-blends in hearing, native signers of American Sign Language. – *SLStud* 11/2, 2010, 205-240.

10.2.3.   LANGUAGE CONTACT

593   Lucas, Ceil; Bayley, Robert; McCaskill, Carolyn; Hill, Joseph: The
       intersection of African American English and Black American Sign
       Language. – *IJB* 19/2, 2015, 156-168.

11.1.   HISTORICAL LINGUISTICS AND LANGUAGE CHANGE

594   Shaw, Emily; Delaporte, Yves: New perspectives on the history of
       American Sign Language. – *SLStud* 11/2, 2010, 158-204.
595   Supalla, Ted; Clark, Patricia: *Sign language archaeology : understand-
       ing the historical roots of American Sign Language.* – Washington,
       D.C. : Gallaudet UP., 2014. – viii, 270 p.
596   Supalla, Ted: The role of historical research in building a model of
       Sign Language typology, variation, and change. – (6), 15-42.

12.3.   COMPUTATIONAL LINGUISTICS

597   Wolfe, Rosalee; Cook, Peter; McDonald, John C.; Schnepp, Jerry:
       Linguistics as structure in computer animation : toward a more effec-
       tive synthesis of brow motion in American Sign Language. – *SLLing*
       14/1, 2011, 179-199.

2. Individual sign languages (except ASL)

598   Adone, Marie Carla D.; Maypilama, Elaine L. : *A grammar sketch of
       Yoḻŋu Sign Language.* – München : LINCOM Europa, 2014. – viii, 133
       p. – (LINCOM studies in Australian languages ; 8).
599   Angoua Jean-Jacques, Tano: *Etude d'une langue des signes émer-
       gente de Côte d'Ivoire : l'exemple de la Langue des Signes de Bouakako
       (LaSiBo).* – Utrecht : LOT, 2016. – 396 p. – (LOT dissertation series ;
       437) | [The description of an emerging sign language in Ivory Coast :
       the Bouakako Sign Language] | Fr. ab | E. summary p. 367-374 | Du.
       summary p. 375-383.
600   Aronoff, Mark; Meir, Irit; Padden, Carol A.; Sandler, Wendy: The roots
       of linguistic organization in a new language. – (116), 133-152.
601   [Aslan, Sema] Aslan Demir, Sema: Sessizliğin dili : Türk İşaret Dili'ne
       dair gözlemler. – (615), 141-155 | [The language of silence : observations
       on the Turkish Sign Language].

602   Baker, Anne Edith: Poetry in South African Sign Language : what is
      different? – *SPIL* 48, 2017, 87-92 | E. ab.

603   Baker, Anne Edith: Sign languages as natural languages. – (633),
      1-24.

604   Bank, Richard: *The ubiquity of mouthings in NGT : a corpus study.* –
      Utrecht : LOT, 2015. – xi, 153 p. – (LOT dissertation series ; 376) | Du.
      summary, p. 143-151 | Diss. (2015) at the Radboud Univ. Nijmegen | NGT
      = *Nederlandse Gebarentaal* = Dutch Sign Language.

605   Bank, Richard: The ubiquity of mouthings in NGT : a corpus study
      (Radboud University, Nijmegen, 2015). – *SLLing* 18/2, 2015, 257-265 |
      NGT = *Nederlandse Gebarentaal* = Dutch Sign Language | Diss. ab |
      Diss. (2015), cf. 604.

606   Bauer, Anastasia: *The use of signing space in a shared sign language
      of Australia.* – Berlin : De Gruyter Mouton ; Lancaster : Ishara Press,
      2014. – xxiv, 279 p. – (Sign language typology ; 5).

607   Bauer, Anastasia: The use of signing space in a shared sign language of
      Australia : (University of Cologne, 2013). – *SLLing* 17/2, 2014, 259-266 |
      Diss. ab.

608   Brynjólfsdóttir, Elísa Guðrún; Jónsson, Jóhannes Gísli; Þorvaldsdóttir,
      Kristín Lena; Sverrisdóttir, Rannveig: Málfræði íslenska táknmálsins. –
      ÍMAM 34, 2012, 9-52 | E. ab.: The grammar of Icelandic Sign Language.

609   Checchetto, Alessandra; Cecchetto, Carlo; Geraci, Carlo; Guasti, Maria
      Teresa; Zucchi, Alessandro: Una varietà molto speciale : la LISt (lingua
      dei segni italiana tattile). – (621), 207-218.

610   Cieśla, Bartłomiej: Językowe własności systemu komunikacji
      głuchych. – *FLŁ* 46, 2012, 53-59 | E. ab.: Linguistic features of the Polish
      sign lg.

611   Conte, Genny; Santoro, Mirko; Geraci, Carlo; Cardinaletti, Anna:
      Perché alzi le sopracciglia? : le funzioni linguistiche marcate dal sol-
      levamento in LIS. – (621), 161-170.

612   Cruz-Aldrete, Miroslava: Gramática de la Lengua de Señas Mexicana
      (LSM) (El Colegio de México, Mexico City, 2008). – *SLLing* 13/2, 2010,
      241-252 | Abstract of the author's doctoral diss.

613   *Current directions in Turkish sign language research* / Ed. by Engin
      Arik. – Newcastle : Cambridge scholars, 2013. – xix, 306 p. | Not
      analyzed.

614   Davis, Jeffrey E.: *Hand talk : sign language among American Indian
      nations.* – Cambridge : Cambridge UP, 2010. – xxix, 244 p.

615   *Ellerle konuşmak : Türk İşaret Dili araştırmaları* / Derleyen Engin
      Arık. – İstanbul : Koç Üniversitesi Yayınları, 2016. – 540 p. – (Koç

Üniversitesi Yayınları ; 81) | [To speak with the hands : research on the Turkish Sign Language].

616   Erlenkamp, Sonja: Norsk tegnspråk : helt norsk og veldig annerledes : skisse av en ny beskrivelsesmodell for norsk tegnspråk. – *NLT* 29/1, 2011, 26-37 | Norwegian Sign Language : entirely Norwegian and completely different : a sketch for a new descriptive model of Norwegian Sign Language | E. ab.

617   Fabisiak, Sylwia: Imitacyjność w polskim języku migowym. – *PJ* 6, 2010, 62-79 | E. ab.: Imitativeness in Polish sign lg.

618   Fabisiak, Sylwia: Przejawy imitacyjności w systemie gramatycznym Polskiego Języka Migowego. – *LingVaria* 5/1 (9), 2010, 183-192 | E. ab.: Imitative aspects of grammatical system in Polish Sign Language.

619   Fox Tree, Erich: Meemul Tziij : an indigenous sign language complex of Mesoamerica. – *SLStud* 9/3, 2009, 324-366.

620   Gesser, Audrei: *Libras? Que língua é essa? : crenças e preconceitos em torno da língua de sinais e da realidade surda.* – São Paulo : Parábola, 2009. – 87 p. – (Estratégias de ensino ; 14) | Libras? What kind of language is that? : beliefs and prejudices about sign language and the deaf reality.

621   *Grammatica, lessico e dimensioni di variazione nella Lis* | A cura di Anna Cardinaletti ; Carlo Cecchetto ; Caterina Donati. – Milano : FrancoAngeli, 2011. – 272 p. | Lis = Lingua italiana dei segni.

622   Green, Jennifer; Wilkins, David P.: With or without speech : Arandic Sign Language from Central Australia. – *AJL* 34/2, 2014, 234-261.

623   *Handbuch Deutsche Gebärdensprache : sprachwissenschaftliche und anwendungsbezogene Perspektiven* | Hanna Eichmann ; Martje Hansen und Jens Heßmann (Hg.). – Seedorf : Signum, 2012. – xvi, 528 p. – (Internationale Arbeiten zur Gebärdensprache und Kommunikation Gehörloser = International studies on sign language and communication of the Deaf ; 50).

624   Hein, Kadri: The Estonian deaf community. – *SLStud* 10/3, 2010, 304-316.

625   Hendriks, Bernadet: Jordanian Sign Language : aspects of grammar from a cross-linguistic perspective (University of Amsterdam, 2008). – *SLLing* 12/1, 2009, 101-110.

626   Hochgesang, Julie A.; Mcauliff, Kate: An initial description of the Deaf community in Haiti and Haitian Sign Language (LSH). – *SLStud* 16/2, 2016, 227-294 | E. ab.

627   *Indian Sign Language(s)* | G. N. Devy (chief ed.) ; Tanmoy Bhattacharya ; Nisha Grover ; Surinder P. K. Randhawa (eds.). – New

Delhi : Orient Blackswan, 2014. – xli, 198 p. – (People's linguistic survey of India ; 38).

628   *International Sign : linguistic, usage, and status issues* / Rachel Rosenstock and Jemina Napier, editors. – Washington, D.C. : Gallaudet UP., 2016. – 232 p. – (Sociolinguistics in deaf communities ; 21) | Not analyzed.

629   Kendon, Adam: *Sign languages of aboriginal Australia : cultural, semiotic, and communicative perspectives.* – Cambridge : Cambridge UP, 1988. – xviii, 542 p.

630   Korol´kova, Ol´ga O.: Koncepcija postroenija grammatičeskoj sistemy russkogo žestovogo jazyka (k postanovke problemy). – *SFŽ* 4, 2011, 226-233 | On the concept of the construction of a grammatical system for Russian Sign Language.

631   Lackner, Andrea: Linguistic functions of head and body movements in Austrian Sign Language (ÖGS) : a corpus-based analysis (Karl-Franzens-University Graz, 2013). – *SLLing* 18/1, 2015, 151-157 | Diss. ab.

632   Leeson, Lorraine; Saeed, John Ibrahim: *Irish Sign Language : a cognitive linguistic account.* – Edinburgh : Edinburgh UP., 2012. – xii, 244 p.

633   *The linguistics of sign languages : an introduction* / Ed. by Anne Baker ; Beppie van den Bogaerde ; Roland Pfau ; Trude Schermer. – Amsterdam : Benjamins, 2016. – xv, 378 p.

634   Lutalo-Kiingi, Sam: The importance of Deaf involvement in African Sign Language research. – (18), 23-27.

635   Marsaja, I Gede: *Desa Kolok : a deaf village and its sign language in Bali, Indonesia.* – Nijmegen : Ishara Press, 2008. – xxi, 262 p., 1 DVD | Revised version of the author's 2003 La Trobe Univ. diss.

636   Nyst, Victoria: Sign languages in West Africa. – (218), 405-432.

637   Nyst, Victoria; Sylla, Kara; Magassouba, Moustapha: Deaf signers in Douentza, a rural area in Mali. – (1047), 251-276.

638   *Polski język migowy : konwersacje* / Red. Agnieszka Kwiecień ; Olga Romanowska. – Łódź : Polski Związek Głuchych Oddział Łódzki, 2011. – 100 p., DVD | Polish sign language : conversations.

639   Quer, Josep: La llengua de signes catalana, una llengua pròpia més de Catalunya. – *CatRev* 24, 2010 [2011], 45-57.

640   Rutkowski, Paweł; Łozińska, Sylwia: O niedookreśloności semantycznej migowych predykatów klasyfikatorowych. – (45), 211-223 | E. ab.: On the semantic underspecification of sign lg. classifier predicates.

641   Sanjabi, Ali; Behmanesh, Abbas Ali; Guity, Ardavan; Siyavoshi, Sara; Watkins, Martin; Hochgesang, Julie A.: Zaban Eshareh Irani (ZEI) and its fingerspelling system. – *SLStud* 16/4, 2016, 500-534 | E. ab.

642   Sawicka, Grażyna: Polski Język Migowy (PJM) : język czy nie język?. –
      (197), 83-88.

643   Schmaling, Constanze H.: Hausa Sign language. – (219), 361-389.

644   Schmaling, Halima C.; Hausawa, Lawan Bala: *Maganar Hannu :
      Harshen Bebaye na Kasar Hausa.* Littafi na Farko *Iyali.* – Kano :
      Goethe Institut, 2011. – 28 p. | Sign language : the language of the Deaf
      in Hausaland : Book one : Family.

645   Szabó, Mária Helga: A hangzó magyar nyelv hatása a magyar jelny-
      elvre. – (16), 43-79 | The effect of sounding Hungarian on Hungarian
      Sign Language.

646   Szczepankowski, Bogdan; Koncewicz, Dorota: *Język migowy w terapii.*
      – Łódź : Wyd. Naukowe Wyższej Szkoły Pedagogicznej w Łodzi, 2012.
      – 241 p., CD-ROM/DVD | Sign language in therapy.

647   Tano, Angoua Jean-Jacques: Etude d'une langue des signes émergente
      de Côte d'Ivoire : l'exemple de la Langue des Signes de Bouakako
      (LaSiBo). – *SLLing* 20/1, 2017, 146-155 | [Study of an emerging sign lan-
      guage in Ivory Coast : the example of the Bouakako Sign Language
      (LaSiBo)] | Diss. ab.

648   *Through Indian* Sign Language : the Fort Sill ledgers of Hugh Lenox
      Scott and Iseeo, 1889-1897 / Ed. by William C. Meadows. – Norman,
      OK : Univ. of Oklahoma Press, 2015. – 520 p. – (The civilization of the
      American Indian series ; 274).

649   Tomaszewski, Piotr; Piekot, Tomasz: Język migowy w perspektywie
      socjolingwistycznej. – *Socjolingwistyka* 29, 2015, 63-87 | Sign language
      from sociolinguistic perspective | Pol. & E. ab.

650   Vonen, Arnfinn Muruvik: Tegnspråk i Norden. – *SpriN* 2012, 86-96 |
      Sign languages in the Nordic countries | E. & Norw. ab.

651   Vos, Connie de: Sign-spatiality in Kata Kolok : how a village sign lan-
      guage of Bali inscribes its signing space. – *SLLing* 16/2, 2013, 277-284 |
      Diss. ab.

652   Wojda, Piotr: Naturalne języki migowe a polski język migowy. – (172),
      372-391 | Natural sign languages and Polish sign language | Pol. & E. ab.

653   Wrobel, Ulrike Rosa: Raum als kommunikative Ressource – eine han-
      dlungstheoretische Analyse visueller Sprachen. – *SLLing* 10/2, 2008,
      223-231 | Space as a communicative resource – a functional-pragmatic
      approach to visual languages | Ab. of the author's diss.

654   [Wrzesniewska, Marta] Wrześniewska-Pietrzak, Marta; Ruta,
      Karolina: Rzecz o nieobecnych : o słownikach polskiego języka
      migowego. – *PF* 65, 2014, 359-376 | E. ab.: On the absent ones: diction-
      aries of the Polish sign lg.

655   Zeshan, Ulrike: Village sign languages : a commentary. – (203), 13 p. |
      Cf. 826.

656   Zwets, Martine: *Locating the difference : a comparison between
      Dutch pointing gestures and pointing signs in Sign Language of the
      Netherlands.* – Utrecht : LOT, 2014. – iv, 219 p. – (LOT dissertation
      series ; 351) | Du. summary, p. 207-216 | Diss.

0.3.   LINGUISTIC THEORY AND METHODOLOGY

657   Bōnō, Mayumi: Nihon shuwa danwa ni okeru kūkan to shiten : shuwa
      kenkyū to jesuchā kenkyū no setten. – *ShK* 17, 2008, 1-10 | [Space and
      viewpoint in Japan Sign Language discourse : interaction between
      sign language research and gesture research].

658   Davis, Jeffrey E.: American Indian Sign Language : documentary lin-
      guistic methodologies and technologies. – (176), 161-178.

659   Davis, Jeffrey E.: American Indian Sign Language documentary lin-
      guistic fieldwork and digital archive. – (177), 69-82.

660   Dikyuva, Hasan; Escobedo Delgado, César Ernesto; Panda, Sibaji;
      Zeshan, Ulrike: Working with village sign language communities :
      deaf fieldwork researchers in professional dialogue. – (1047), 313-404.

661   Haug, Tobias: A review of sign language acquisition studies as the
      basis for informed decisions for sign language test adaptation : the
      case of the German Sign Language Receptive Skills Test. – *SLLing* 15/2,
      2012, 213-239.

662   Kimura, Tsutomu; Hara, Daisuke; Kanda, Kazuyuki; Morimoto,
      Kazunari: Nihon shuwa, Nihongo jisho shisutemu no hatten to hyōka.
      – *ShK* 17, 2008, 11-27 | [Development and assessment of Japan Sign
      Language and the Japanese dictonary system].

663   Kusters, Annelies: Being a deaf white anthropologist in Adamorobe :
      some ethical and methodological issues. – (1047), 27-52.

664   Lutalo-Kiingi, Sam; Clerck, Goedele A. M. De: Research on sign lan-
      guages and deaf/sign communities in sub-Saharan Africa : challenges
      of diversity, documentation, revitalization, language planning, and
      capacity building. – (20), 354-375.

665   Zeshan, Ulrike; Dikyuva, Hasan: Documentation for endangered sign
      languages : the case of Mardin Sign Language. – (177), 29-41.

0.5.   SEMIOTICS

666   Kutscher, Silvia: Ikonizität und Indexikalität im gebärdensprachli-
       chen Lexikon : zur Typologie sprachlicher Zeichen. – ZS 29/1, 2010,
       79-109 | E. ab.
667   Reis, Marga; Wöllstein, Angelika: Zur Grammatik (vor allem) kondi-
       tionaler V1-Gefüge im Deutschen. – ZS 29/1, 2010, 111-179 | E. ab.

0.5.1.   NON-VERBAL COMMUNICATION

668   Arık, Engin: Left/right and front/back in sign, speech, and co-speech
       gestures : what do data from Turkish Sign Language, Croatian Sign
       Language, American Sign Language, Turkish, Croatian, and English
       reveal? – PSiCL 47/3, 2011, 442-469.
669   Arvensisová,   Marika: Neverbálne   prostriedky   komunikácie
       nepočujúcich a ich špecifiká. – MinV 2/2, 2013, 103-111 | Non-verbal
       communication of the deaf : its means and specifics | E. ab.
670   Barberà, Gemma; Zwets, Martine: Pointing and reference in sign lan-
       guage and spoken language : anchoring vs. identifying. – SLStud 13/4,
       2013, 491-515 | E. ab.
671   Johnston, Trevor; Roekel, Jane van; Schembri, Adam C.: On the con-
       ventionalization of mouth actions in Australian Sign Language. – L&S
       59/1, 2016, 3-42.
672   Mohr, Susanne: Mouth actions in sign languages : an empirical study
       of Irish Sign Language. – Berlin : De Gruyter Mouton ; Preston, UK :
       Ishara Press, 2014. – xviii, 231 p. – (Sign languages and deaf communi-
       ties ; 3).
673   Ōsugi, Yutaka: "Shuwa" kara "shuwa gengo" e. – Nihongogaku 33/11,
       2014, 4-14 | From "signing" to "sign language".
674   Raanes, Eli: Tegnrom og taktilt tegnspråk. – NLT 29/1, 2011, 54-86 |
       Signing space and tactile sign language | E. ab.
675   Rizzi, Mariapia: Manomissioni : tre strategie iconiche del testo
       poetico segnato. – (14), 189-206.

0.6.   APPLIED LINGUISTICS

676   Escuela española de sordomudos : la gramática de la lengua de signos en
       su contexto interlingüístico y pedagógico / Lorenzo Hervás y Panduro :
       estudio introd. y ed. de Ángel Luis Herrero Blanco. – Alicante : Univ.
       de Alicante, 2008. – 407 p.

677   Garncarek, Michał: Polski język migowy w nauczaniu osób słyszących :
      wskazówki metodyczne. – *JwK* 2, 2012, 129-140 | Polish Sign Language
      and its teaching to hearing persons : methodical advices | E. ab.

1.   PHONETICS AND PHONOLOGY

678   [Kimmelman, Vadim] Kimmelman, Vadim; Sáfár, Anna; Crasborn,
      Onno A.: Towards a classification of weak hand holds. – *OpLi* 2/1, 2016,
      211-234 | E. ab.

679   Puupponen, Anna; Wainio, Tuija; Burger, Birgitta; Jantunen, Tommi:
      Head movements in Finnish Sign Language on the basis of motion
      capture data : a study of the form and function of nods, nodding, head
      thrusts, and head pulls. – *SLLing* 18/1, 2015, 41-89.

1.1.   PHONETICS

680   Arendsen, Jeroen; Doorn, Andrea J. van; Ridder, Huib de: Acceptability
      of sign manipulations. – *SLLing* 13/2, 2010, 101-155.

681   Barbosa, Felipe Venâncio; Temoteo, Janice Gonçalves; Nogueira Rizzo,
      Rodrigo Rossi: What generates Location? Study on the arm and fore-
      arm of lexical items in the Brazilian Sign Language. – (32), 181-194 | E. ab.

682   Crasborn, Onno A.: Phonetics. – (633), 229-249.

683   Healy, Christina: Pinky extension as a phonestheme in Mongolian
      Sign Language. – *SLStud* 11/4, 2011, 575-593 | E. ab.

684   Jantunen, Tommi: How long is the sign? – *Linguistics* 53/1, 2015,
      93-124.

685   Ormel, Ellen; Crasborn, Onno A.; Kooij, Els van der: Coarticulation of
      hand height in Sign Language of the Netherlands is affected by con-
      tact type. – *JPhon* 41/3-4, 2013, 156-171.

686   Xavier, André Nogueira; [Barbosa, Plinio Almeida] Barbosa, Plínio:
      Com quantas mãos se faz um sinal? : um estudo do parâmetro
      número de mãos na produção de sinais da língua brasileira de sinais
      (libras). – *TAL-RLL* 15/1, 2013, 111-128 | How many hands do you need to
      make a sign? : on the parameter "number of hands" in producing signs
      in Brazilian Sign Language (Libras) | E. ab.

1.1.1.   ARTICULATORY PHONETICS

687   Geraci, Carlo: Epenthesis in Italian Sign Language. – *SLLing* 12/1, 2009,
      3-51.

1.2. PHONOLOGY

688   Borstell, Carl; Lepic, Ryan: Commentary on Kita, van Gijn & van der
      Hulst (1998). – *SLLing* 17/2, 2014, 241-250 | Comm. on an unpublished
      manuscript from 1998, publ. in 2014 as 697.

689   Brentari, Diane K.; Eccarius, Petra: Handshape contrasts in sign lan-
      guage phonology. – (218), 284-311.

690   Demey, Eline; Kooij, Els van der: Phonological patterns in a depen-
      dency model : allophonic relations grounded in phonetic and iconic
      motivation. – *Lingua* 118/8, 2008, 1109-1138.

691   Elliott, Eeva A.; Jacobs, Arthur M.: Phonological and morphological
      faces : disgust signs in German Sign Language. – *SLLing* 17/2, 2014,
      123-180.

692   Fenlon, Jordan; Schembri, Adam C.; Rentelis, Ramas; Cormier, Kearsy:
      Variation in handshape and orientation in British Sign Language : the
      case of the '1' hand configuration. – *L&C* 33/1, 2013, 69-91.

693   Giustolisi, Beatrice; Mereghetti, Emiliano; Cecchetto, Carlo:
      Phonological blending or code mixing? : why mouthing is not a core
      component of sign language grammar. – *NLLT* 35/2, 2017, 347-365 |
      E. ab.

694   *Handbuch Laut, Gebärde, Buchstabe* / Hrsg. von Ulrike Domahs und
      Beatrice Primus. – Berlin : De Gruyter Mouton, 2016. – xx, 516 p. –
      (Handbücher Sprachwissen ; 2) | Handbook of sounds, signs, and
      letters.

695   Jantunen, Tommi; Takkinen, Ritva: Syllable structure in sign language
      phonology. – (218), 312-331.

696   Kimmel′man, Vadim I.: Parts of speech in Russian Sign Language : the
      role of iconicity and economy. – *SLLing* 12/2, 2009, 161-186.

697   [Kita, Sotaro 01] Kita, Sotaro; Gijn, Ingeborg van; Hulst, Harry van
      der: The non-linguistic status of the Symmetry Condition in signed
      languages : evidence from a comparison of signs and speech-accom-
      panying representational gestures. – *SLLing* 17/2, 2014, 215-238 | Cf.
      authors' preface (p. 213-214) and afterword (p. 239-240) | Comm.
      cf. 688.

698   Köhlo, Mikhaela D. K.; Siebörger, Ian; Bennett, William G.: A perfect
      end : a study of syllable codas in South African Sign Language. –
      SPILPLUS 52, 2017, 127-156 | E. ab.

699   Kooij, Els van der: Phonology. – (633), 251-278.

700   Kozak, L. Viola; Tomita, Nozomi: On selected phonological patterns in
      Saudi Arabian Sign Language. – *SLStud* 13/1, 2012, 56-78 | E. ab.

701 Lee, Hsin-hsien: The representation of handshape change in Taiwan Sign Language. – *SLLing* 11/2, 2008, 139-183.

702 Lewin, Donna; Schembri, Adam C.: Mouth gestures in British Sign Language : a case study of tongue protrusion in BSL narratives. – *SLLing* 14/1, 2011, 94-114.

703 Makaroğlu, Bahtiyar; Bekar, İpek Pınar; Arık, Engin: Evidence for minimal pairs in Turkish Sign Language (TİD). – *PSiCL* 50/3, 2014, 207-230 | E. ab.

704 Nishio, Rie: Kōpasu ni motozuku shuwa on'inron no kenkyū : Doitsu shuwa ni okeru weak drop to weak prop ni tsuite. – *ShK* 18, 2009, 47-60 | [Sign language phonology research based on a corpus : weak drop and weak prop in German Sign Language].

705 Özkul, Aslı: Türk İşaret Dilinde araç bildiren isim ve fiil çiftlerine birimbilimsel bir bakış. – (615), 211-230 | [A look into the phonology of instrumental nouns and verbs in Turkish Sign Language].

706 Richterová, Klára: O vzdálených i blízkých aspektech fonologie znakového jazyka : nepříznakové tvary ruky (nejen) v českém znakovém jazyce. – (1), 99-112 | On distant and near aspects of sign language phonology : unmarked hand shapes (not only) in Czech Sign Language | Pol. & G. ab.

707 Sandler, Wendy; Aronoff, Mark; Meir, Irit; Padden, Carol A.: The gradual emergence of phonological form in a new language. – *NLLT* 29/2, 2011, 503-543 | On Al-Sayyid Bedouin Sign Language.

708 Stoianov, Diane; Nevins, Andrew Ira: The phonology of handshape distribution in Maxakalí sign. – (40), 231-262 | E. ab.

709 Sze, Felix Yim Binh: Nonmanual markings for topic constructions in Hong Kong Sign Language. – *SLLing* 14/1, 2011, 115-147.

710 Yang, Junhui: Numeral signs and compounding in Chinese Sign Language (CSL). – (300), 253-268.

1.2.1. SUPRASEGMENTAL PHONOLOGY (PROSODY)

711 Bank, Richard; Crasborn, Onno A.; Hout, Roeland van: Alignment of two languages : the spreading of mouthings in Sign Language of the Netherlands. – *IJB* 19/1, 2015, 40-55.

712 Crasborn, Onno A.; Kooij, Els van der: The phonology of focus in Sign Language of the Netherlands. – *JL* 49/3, 2013, 515-565.

713 Crasborn, Onno A.; Kooij, Els van der; Ros, Johan: On the weight of phrase-final prosodic words in a sign language. – *SLLing* 15/1, 2012, 11-38.

714   Dachkovsky, Svetlana: Facial expression as intonation in Israeli Sign
       Language : the case of neutral and counterfactual conditionals. – (30),
       61-82.

715   Dachkovsky, Svetlana; Healy, Christina; Sandler, Wendy: Visual into-
       nation in two sign languages. – *Phonology* 30/2, 2013, 211-252 | On
       Israeli Sign Language and American Sign Language.

716   Dachkovsky, Svetlana; Sandler, Wendy: Visual intonation in the pros-
       ody of a sign language. – *L&S* 52/2-3, 2009, 287-314.

717   Göksel, Aslı; Kelepir, Meltem; [Untak, Asli] Üntak-Tarhan, Aslı:
       Decomposing the non-manual tier : cross-modality generalisations.
       – *BLS* 35S, 2009 (2010), 1-11 | Evidence from Turkish and Turkish Sign
       Language.

718   Herrmann, Annika: The interaction of eye blinks and other prosodic
       cues in German Sign Language. – *SLLing* 13/1, 2010, 3-39.

719   Herrmann, Annika: Prosody in German Sign Language. – (23),
       349-380.

720   Jantunen, Tommi: Acceleration peaks and sonority in Finnish Sign
       Language syllables. – (87), 347-381.

721   Kooij, Els van der; Crasborn, Onno A.: Syllables and the word-prosodic
       system in Sign Language of the Netherlands. – *Lingua* 118/9, 2008,
       1307-1327.

722   Özsoy, A. Sumru; Kelepir, Meltem; Nuhbalaoğlu, Derya; Hakgüder,
       Emre: Commands in Turkish sign language. – *GK* 146, 2014, 13-30 | Jap.
       ab.

723   Quer, Josep: Intonation and grammar in the visual-gestural modality :
       a case study on conditionals in Catalan Sign Language (LSC). – (190),
       369-386.

724   Sandler, Wendy; Meir, Irit; Dachkovsky, Svetlana; Padden, Carol A.;
       Aronoff, Mark: The emergence of complexity in prosody and syntax. –
       Lingua 121/13, 2011, 2014-2033.

725   Sze, Felix Yim Binh: Blinks and intonational phrasing in Hong Kong
       Sign Language. – (30), 83-107.

726   Tang, Gladys; Brentari, Diane K.; González, Carolina; Sze, Felix Yim
       Binh: Crosslinguistic variation in prosodic cues. – (218), 519-542.

727   Vos, Connie de; Kooij, Els van der; Crasborn, Onno A.: Mixed sig-
       nals : combining linguistic and affective functions of eyebrows in
       questions in Sign Language of the Netherlands. – *L&S* 52/2-3, 2009,
       315-339.

1.3.   MOR(PHO)PHONOLOGY

728   Brentari, Diane K.; Coppola, Marie; Mazzoni, Laura; Goldin-Meadow,
      Susan: When does a system become phonological? : handshape pro-
      duction in gesturers, signers, and homesigners. – *NLLT* 30/1, 2012, 1-31
      | On Italian & American Sign Language.

2.   GRAMMAR, MORPHOSYNTAX

729   Antzakas, Klimis: Aspects of morphology and syntax of negation in
      Greek Sign Language (City University London, 2008). – *SLLing* 11/2,
      2008, 265-275 | Abstract of the author's diss.

730   Arık, Engin: Türk İşaret Dili'nde sınıflandırıcılar üzerine bir çalışma. –
      Bilig 67, 2013, 1–24 | On classifiers in Turkish sign language.

731   Baker, Anne Edith; Pfau, Roland: Constituents and word classes. –
      (633), 93-115.

732   Benedicto, Elena E.; Cvejanov, Sandra; Quer, Josep: The morphosyntax
      of verbs of motion in serial constructions : a crosslinguistic study in
      three signed languages. – (30), 111-132.

733   Cormier, Kearsy; Fenlon, Jordan: Possession in the visual-gestural
      modality : how possession is expressed in British Sign Language. –
      (88), 389-422.

734   Cormier, Kearsy; Fenlon, Jordan; Schembri, Adam C.: Indicating verbs
      in British Sign Language favour motivated use of space. – *OpLi* 1/1,
      2015, 684-707 | Electronic publ.

735   Crasborn, Onno A.; Kooij, Els van der; Ros, Johan; Hoop, Helen de:
      Topic agreement in NGT (Sign Language of the Netherlands). – *LRev*
      26/2-3, 2009, 355-370.

736   Duarte, Kyle: The mechanics of fingerspelling : analyzing Ethiopian
      Sign Language. – *SLStud* 11/1, 2010, 5-21.

737   Garcia, Brigitte; Sallandre, Marie-Anne: Reference resolution in
      French Sign Language (LSF). – (100), 316-364.

738   Haviland, John B.: The emerging grammar of nouns in a first gen-
      eration sign language : specification, iconicity, and syntax. – (221),
      65-110.

739   Hosemann, Jana: Eye gaze and verb agreement in German Sign
      Language : a first glance. – *SLLing* 14/1, 2011, 76-93 | Compared
      to ASL.

740   Hunsicker, Dea; Goldin-Meadow, Susan: How handshape type can
      distinguish between nouns and verbs in homesign. – (221), 111-133.

741   Imazato, Noriko: Nihon shuwa ni okeru shugo/mokutekigo hyōji no
      jodōshi ni tsuite. – *GK* 146, 2014, 31-50 | E. ab.: Subject/object marking
      auxiliaries in Japanese sign languages.

742   Johnston, Trevor: Formational and functional characteristics of
      pointing signs in a corpus of Auslan (Australian sign language) :
      are the data sufficient to posit a grammatical class of 'pronouns' in
      Auslan? – *CLLT* 9/1, 2013, 109-159 | E. ab.

743   Klann, Juliane: *Ikonizität in Gebärdensprachen.* – Berlin : De Gruyter
      Mouton, 2014. – xv, 167 p. – (Linguistik – Impulse & Tendenzen ; 59).

744   Ktejik, Mish: Numeral incorporation in Japanese Sign Language. –
      SLStud 13/2, 2013, 186-210 | E. ab.

745   Lutalo-Kiingi, Sam: A descriptive grammar of morphosyntactic con-
      structions in Ugandan Sign Language (UgSL). – *SLLing* 19/1, 2016, 132-
      141 | Diss. ab. (University of Central Lancashire, 2014).

746   Meir, Irit: The emergence of argument structure in two new sign lan-
      guages. – (13), 101-123 | On Israeli Sign Language (ISL) and Al-Sayyid
      Bedouin Sign Language (ABSL).

747   Meir, Irit: The evolution of verb classes and verb agreement in sign
      languages. – *TL* 38/1-2, 2012, 145-152 | Comm. on 265 | Response cf. 267.

748   Rinfret, Julie: The spatial association of nouns in *Langue des Signes
      Québécoise* : form, function and meaning (Université du Québec à
      Montréal, 2009). – *SLLing* 13/1, 2010, 92-97 | Abstract of the author's
      doctoral diss.

749   Rutkowski, Paweł; Czajkowski-Kisil, Małgorzata: O kategorii zaimka
      osobowego w polskim języku migowym (PJM). – *LingVaria* 5/1 (9),
      2010, 65-77 | E. ab.: On the category of personal pronouns in Polish
      Sign Language.

750   Sevinç, Ayça Müge; Bozşahin, Cem: Verbal categories in Turkish sign
      language. – (35), 220-229.

751   Tkachman, Oksana; Sandler, Wendy: The noun-verb distinction in
      two young sign languages. – (221), 9-41.

2.1.   MORPHOLOGY AND WORD-FORMATION

752   Brunelli, Michele: Antisymmetry and sign languages : a compari-
      son between NGT and LIS (University of Amsterdam & Ca'Foscari
      University, Venice, 2011). – *SLLing* 15/1, 2012, 175-183 | Abstract of the
      author's diss. (780).

753   Damian, Simona: An introduction to the morphology of Romanian
      sign language. – *StUBB-Ph* 56/1, 2011, 133-138 | E. ab.

754 [Hudson, Carla L.] Hudson Kam, Carla L.; [Goodrich, Whitney]
     Goodrich Smith, Whitney: The problem of conventionality in the
     development of creole morphological systems. – *CJL* 56/1, 2011, 109-
     124 | On spatial morphology in Nicaraguan Sign Language.

755 Morris, Carla D.; Schneider, Erin: On selected morphemes in Saudi
     Arabian Sign Language. – *SLStud* 13/1, 2012, 103-121 | E. ab.

756 Pfau, Roland: Morphology. – (633), 197-228.

757 Sagara, Keiko: Aspects of number and kinship terms in Japanese Sign
     Language. – (300), 301-331.

2.1.1.   INFLECTIONAL MORPHOLOGY

758 [Antzakas, Klimis] Ἀντζακας, Κλήμης; Quer, Josep: Η ρηματική
     συμφωνία στην ελληνική νοηματική γλώσσα. – *SGL* 35, 2015, 92-105 | Verb
     agreement in Greek Sign Language.

759 Crasborn, Onno A.; Kooij, Els van der; Waters, Dafydd; Woll, Bencie;
     Mesch, Johanna: Frequency distribution and spreading behavior of
     different types of mouth actions in three sign languages. – *SLLing* 11/1,
     2008, 45-67.

760 Lam, Scholastica Wai-sze: Reconsidering number agreement in Hong
     Kong Sign Language. – (30), 133-160.

761 Maxaroblidze, Tamar: versiis k'at'egoria kartul žest'ur enaši. –
     k'admosi 5, 2013, 168-191 | E. ab.: The category of version in Georgian
     Sign Language.

762 Morgan, Hope E.; Mayberry, Rachel I.: Complexity in two-handed
     signs in Kenyan Sign Language : evidence for sublexical structure in a
     young sign language. – *SLLing* 15/1, 2012, 147-174.

763 Zwitserlood, Inge: Morphology below the level of the sign : "frozen"
     forms and classifier predicates. – (30), 251-272.

2.1.2.   DERIVATIONAL MORPHOLOGY

764 Fuentes, Mariana; Massone, María Ignacia; Fernández Viader, M. Pilar;
     Makotrinsky, Alejandro; Pulgarin, Francisca: Numeral-incorporating
     roots in numeral systems : a comparative analysis of two sign lan-
     guages. – *SLStud* 11/1, 2010, 55-75.

765 Herlofsky, William J.: Iconic thinking and the contact-induced trans-
     fer of linguistic material : the case of Japanese, signed Japanese, and
     Japan Sign Language. – (73), 19-38.

766 Podstolec, Alicja: Różnice w sposobach derywacji między pols-
kim językiem mówionym a miganym. – (22), 126-131 | Differences
between Polish spoken lg. and the Polish Sign Language in the field of
derivation.

767 Young, Lesa; Palmer, Jeffrey Levi; Reynolds, Wanette: Selected lexical
patterns in Saudi Arabian Sign Language. – *SLStud* 13/1, 2012, 79-102 |
E. ab.

2.2. SYNTAX

768 [Antzakas, Klimis] Άντζακας, Κλήμης: Το πεδίο εμβέλειας της άρνησης
στην ελληνική νοηματική γλώσσα. – (9), 635-645 | E. ab.

769 Barberà, Gemma; Cabredo Hofherr, Patricia: Backgrounded agents in
Catalan Sign Language (LSC) : passives, middles, or impersonals? –
Language 93/4, 2017, 767-798 | E. ab.

770 Barros, Courtney de; Siebörger, Ian: Sentential negation in South
African Sign Language : a case study. – *Literator* 37/2, 2016, 13 p. | E. &
Afrikaans ab.

771 Bertone, Carmela; Cardinaletti, Anna: Il sistema pronominale della
lingua dei segni italiana. – (621), 145-160.

772 Borstell, Carl: Object marking in the signed modality : verbal and
nominal strategies in Swedish Sign Language and other sign lan-
guages. – *SLLing* 20/2, 2017, 279-287 | Diss. ab.

773 Bos, Heleen F.: Serial verb constructions in Sign Language of the
Netherlands. – *SLLing* 19/2, 2016, 238-251 | Paper presented at the Fifth
International Conference on Theoretical Issues in Sign Language
Research (TISLR) in Montreal, Canada (September 1996).

774 Branchini, Chiara; Cardinaletti, Anna; Cecchetto, Carlo; Donati,
Caterina; Geraci, Carlo: wh-duplication in Italian Sign Language (LIS).
– *SLLing* 16/2, 2013, 157-188.

775 Branchini, Chiara; Donati, Caterina: Relatively different : Italian Sign
Language relative clauses in a typological perspective. – (99), 157-191.

776 Branchini, Chiara; Geraci, Carlo: L'ordine dei costituenti in LIS : risul-
tati preliminari. – (621), 113-126.

777 Branchini, Chiara: On relativization and clefting in Italian Sign
Language. – *SLLing* 10/2, 2008, 201-212 | Ab. of the author's diss.

778 Branchini, Chiara: *On relativization and clefting : an analysis of Italian
Sign Language.* – Berlin : De Gruyter Mouton, 2014. – xvii, 343 p. –
(Sign languages and deaf communities ; 5).

779   Bross, Fabian; Hole, Daniel: Scope-taking strategies and the order of
      clausal categories in German Sign Language. – *Glossa* 2/1, 2017, 76 |
      E. ab.

780   Brunelli, Michele: *Antisymmetry and sign languages : a comparison
      between NGT and LIS.* – Utrecht : LOT, 2011. – 348 p. – (LOT disserta-
      tion series ; 284) | Amsterdam Univ. diss | Du. & It. ab | Cf. 752.

781   Brynjólfsdóttir, Elísa Guðrún; Þorvaldsdóttir, Kristín Lena: Að tengja
      saman epli og appelsínur : aðaltengingar í íslenska táknmálinu. –
      ÍMAM 36, 2014, 127-137 | E. ab.: Connecting apples and oranges : con-
      junctions in Icelandic Sign Language.

782   Cecchetto, Carlo; Checchetto, Alessandra; Geraci, Carlo; Santoro,
      Mirko; [Zucchi, Alessandro] Zucchi, Sandro: The syntax of predicate
      ellipsis in Italian Sign Language (LIS). – *Lingua* 166/B, 2015, 214-235.

783   Cecchetto, Carlo; Donati, Caterina: Relativization in Italian Sign
      Language : the missing link of relativization. – (289), 182-203 | E. ab.

784   Costello, Brendan: Language and modality : effects of the use of space
      in the agreement system of *lengua de signos española* (Spanish Sign
      Language). – *SLLing* 19/2, 2016, 270-279 | Diss. ab.

785   Donati, Caterina; Barberà, Gemma; Branchini, Chiara; Cecchetto,
      Carlo; Geraci, Carlo; Quer, Josep: Searching for imperatives in
      European sign languages. – (104), 111-155 | E. ab.

786   Donati, Caterina; Branchini, Chiara: Challenging linearization : simul-
      taneous mixing in the production of bimodal bilinguals. – (98), 93-128
      | A case study of Italian Sign Language-Italian bilinguals.

787   Erlenkamp, Sonja: Grunntegnstilling i norsk tegnspråk. – *NLT* 29/1,
      2011, 87-116 | Basic sign order in Norwegian Sign Language | E. ab.

788   Ferrara, Lindsay; Johnston, Trevor: Elaborating who's what : a study
      of constructed action and clause structure in Auslan (Australian Sign
      Language). – *AJL* 34/2, 2014, 193-215.

789   Geraci, Carlo; Aristodemo, Valentina: An in-depth tour into sentential
      complementation in Italian Sign Language. – (289), 95-150 | E. ab.

790   Geraci, Carlo; Bayley, Robert: Chi, cosa, dove, perché, quando : la dis-
      tribuzione dei segni wh- in LIS. – (621), 127-144.

791   Geraci, Carlo; Cecchetto, Carlo: Neglected cases of rightward move-
      ment : when wh-phrases and negative quantifiers go to the right. –
      (25), 211-241.

792   Gil, David: Sign languages, creoles, and the development of predica-
      tion. – (185), 37-64.

793   Gökgöz, Kadir: Negation in Turkish Sign Language : the syntax of non-
      manual markers. – *SLLing* 14/1, 2011, 49-75.

794   Gökgöz, Kadir; Wilbur, Ronnie B.: Olumsuz evet-hayır sorularında
       olumlu önyargı : Türk İşaret Dili'nde olumsuzluk başından tümleyici
       başa taşımanın delili. – (615), 253-273 | [Positive bias in negative yes-
       no questions : raising from negation to complement in Turkish Sign
       language].

795   Göksel, Aslı; Hakgüder, Emre; Kelepir, Meltem: İşaret dillerinde
       karmaşık tümceleri belirlemek : Türk İşaret Dili (TİD) üzerine bir yön-
       tem ve betimleme çalışması. – (33), 162-169 | To determine complex
       sentences in sign languages : a methodological and descriptive study
       on the basis of Turkish Sign Language.

796   Göksel, Aslı; Kelepir, Meltem: Observations on clausal complementa-
       tion in Turkish Sign Language. – (289), 65-94 | E. ab.

797   Göksel, Aslı; Kelepir, Meltem: The phonological and semantic bifurca-
       tion of the functions of an articulator : HEAD in questions in Turkish
       Sign Language. – SLLing 16/1, 2013, 1-30.

798   Hansen, Martje; Heßmann, Jens: Matching propositional content and
       formal markers : sentence boundaries in a DGS text. – SLLing 10/2,
       2008, 145-175.

799   Hansen, Martje: Warum braucht die Deutsche Gebärdensprache kein
       Passiv? : Verfahren der Markierung semantischer Rollen in der DGS. –
       SLLing 10/2, 2008, 213-222 | Why can German Sign Language (DGS) do
       without a passive construction? Ways of marking semantic roles in
       DGS | Ab. of the author's diss.

800   Herrmann, Annika; Steinbach, Markus: Satztypen und Gebärden-
       sprache. – (192), 786-814 | [Clause types and sign language].

801   Hodge, Gabrielle; Johnston, Trevor: Points, depictions, gestures and
       enactment : partly lexical and non-lexical signs as core elements of
       single clause-like units in Auslan (Australian Sign Language). – AJL
       34/2, 2014, 262-291.

802   Hong, Sung-Eun: Ein empirische Untersuchung zu Kongruenzverben
       in der Koreanischen Gebärdensprache [An empirical investigation of
       agreement verbs in Korean Sign Language] (University of Hamburg,
       2008). – SLLing 12/2, 2009, 228-234 | Abstract of the author's doctoral
       diss.

803   Huddlestone, Kate: A preliminary look at negative constructions in
       South African Sign Language : question-answer clauses. – SPIL 48,
       2017, 93-104 | E. ab.

804   İşsever, Selçuk; Makaroğlu, Bahtiyar: Türk İşaret Dili'nde ne-taşıma. –
       (615), 275-296 | [Wh-movement in Turkish Sign Language].

805   Jantunen, Tommi: Clausal coordination in Finnish Sign Language. –
       SLang 40/1, 2016, 204-234 | E. ab.

806   Jantunen, Tommi: Constructed action, the clause and the nature of
       syntax in Finnish Sign Language. – *OpLi* 3/1, 2017, 65-85 | E. ab.

807   Jantunen, Tommi: Ellipsis in Finnish Sign Language. – *NJL* 36/3, 2013,
       303-323.

808   Jantunen, Tommi: The equative sentence in Finnish Sign Language. –
       SLLing 10/2, 2008, 113-143.

809   Jantunen, Tommi: Fixed and free : the order of the verbal predicate
       and its core arguments in declarative transitive clauses of Finnish
       Sign Language. – *SKY* 21, 2008, 83-123.

810   Jantunen, Tommi: Fixed and NOT free : revisiting the order of the
       main clausal constituents in Finnish Sign Language from a corpus
       perspective. – *SKY* 30, 2017, 137-149 | E. ab.

811   Kimmel′man, Vadim I.: Topics and topic prominence in two sign lan-
       guages. – *JoP* 87, 2015, 156-170.

812   Kimmel′man, Vadim I.: Word order in Russian Sign Language. –
       SLStud 12/3, 2012, 414-445 | E. ab.

813   Krebs, Julia: The syntax and the processing of argument relations in
       Austrian Sign Language (ÖGS). – *SLLing* 20/2, 2017, 288-295 | Diss. ab.

814   Krebs, Julia; Wilbur, Ronnie B.; Roehm, Dietmar: Two agreement
       markers in Austrian Sign Language (ÖGS). – *SLLing* 20/1, 2017, 27-54
       | E. ab.

815   Loos, Cornelia: The syntax and semantics of resultative constructions
       in Deutsche Gebärdensprache (DGS) and American Sign Language
       (ASL). – *SLLing* 20/2, 2017, 296-303 | Diss. ab | Full diss. cf. 816.

816   Loos, Cornelia: *The syntax and semantics of resultative constructions in
       Deutsche Gebärdensprache (DGS) and American Sign Language (ASL).* –
       Austin, TX : Univ. of Texas at Austin, 2017. – xvii, 268 p. | Diss. at Univ.
       of Texas at Austin (2017) | E. ab.

817   [Makharoblidze, Tamara] Makharoblidze, Tamar: Indirect object
       markers in Georgian Sign Language. – *SLLing* 18/2, 2015, 238-250.

818   Mantovan, Lara; Geraci, Carlo: The syntax of nominal modification in
       Italian Sign Language (LIS). – *SLLing* 20/2, 2017, 183-220 | E. ab.

819   Mantovan, Lara: *Nominal modification in Italian Sign Language.* –
       Berlin : De Gruyter Mouton ; Preston, UK : Ishara Press, 2017. – xvii,
       207 p. – (Sign languages and deaf communities ; 8).

820   [McKee, Rachel M Locker] McKee, Rachel; Schembri, Adam C.; McKee,
       David; Johnston, Trevor: Variable "subject" presence in Australian Sign
       Language and New Zealand Sign Language. – *LVC* 23/3, 2011, 375-398.

821 Minoura, Nobukatsu: Inversion in Sayula Popoluca and Japanese Sign Language. – *GKR* 18, 2013, 41-54 | Jap. ab.

822 Minoura, Nobukatsu: Madagasukaru shuwa (TTM) no juekisha ninshō itchi hyōshiki ni kanshite. – *TGDR* 94, 2017, 37-52 | On benefactive person agreement marker in Malagasy sign language (TTM) | Jap. ab.

823 Minoura, Nobukatsu: On S, A, P, T, and R alignment in Malagasy Sign Language (TTM). – *GKR* 19, 2014, 1-20 | Jap. ab.

824 Morgan, Michael W.: Typology of Indian Sign Language verbs from a comparative perspective. – (189), 103-131 | A comparison with British, American & Japanese Sign Language.

825 Müller de Quadros, Ronice; Lillo-Martin, Diane C.: Clause structure. – (218), 225-251.

826 Nonaka, Angela M.: Interrogatives in Ban Khor Sign Language : a preliminary description. – (203), 30 p. | Cf. 655.

827 Pavlič, Matic: Sharing space in Slovenian Sign Language (SZJ). – *GLS* 83, 2015, 67-91.

828 Pfau, Roland; Bos, Heleen F.: Syntax : simple sentences. – (633), 117-147.

829 Pfau, Roland: Syntax : complex sentences. – (633), 149-172.

830 Quer, Josep: Les oracions condicionals en llengua de signes catalana. – (41), Vol. 2, 121-127 | [Conditional clauses in Catalan sign language].

831 Quer, Josep: Reporting with and without role shift : sign language strategies of complementation. – (289), 204-230 | E. ab.

832 Quer, Josep; Rosselló, Joana: On sloppy readings, ellipsis and pronouns : missing arguments in Catalan Sign Language (LSC) and other argument-drop languages. – (111), 337-370.

833 Rosenstock, Rachel: The role of iconicity in international sign. – *SLStud* 8/2, 2008, 131-159.

834 Rutkowski, Paweł; Kuder, Anna; Czajkowski-Kisil, Małgorzata; Łacheta, Joanna: The structure of nominal constructions in Polish Sign Language (PJM) : a corpus-based study. – *SiPL* 10, 2015, 1-15 | E. & Pol. ab.

835 Schwager, Waldemar; Zeshan, Ulrike: Word classes in sign languages : criteria and classifications. – *SLang* 32/3, 2008, 509-545 | Evidence from Kata Kolok (signed in a village in Bali) and German Sign Language.

836 Sprenger, Kristen; Mathur, Gaurav: Observations on word order in Saudi Arabian Sign Language. – *SLStud* 13/1, 2012, 122-134 | E. ab.

837 Sze, Felix Yim Binh: Topic constructions in Hong Kong Sign Language (University of Bristol, 2008). – *SLLing* 12/2, 2009, 222-227 | Abstract of the author's doctoral diss.

838   Uchibori, Asako; Matsuoka, Kazumi: Some observations on wh-
       clauses in Japanese Sign Language. – *JJLing* 29, 2013, 19-30 | E. ab.

839   Uchibori, Asako; Matsuoka, Kazumi: Split movement of wh-elements
       in Japanese Sign Language : a preliminary study. – *Lingua* 183, 2016,
       107-125 | E. ab.

840   Vletsi, Eleni; Stavrakaki, Stavroula: Tense and aspect in Greek Sign
       Language. – (9), 589-600.

841   Weerdt, Danny De: Existential sentences in Flemish Sign Language
       and Finnish Sign Language. – *SKY* 29, 2016, 7-38 | E. ab.

3.   LEXICON (LEXICOLOGY AND LEXICOGRAPHY)

842   Cabeza Pereiro, Carmen: Metaphor and lexicon in sign languages :
       analysis of the hand-opening articulation in LSE and BSL. – *SLStud*
       14/3, 2014, 302-332 | LSE = *lengua de signos española* (Spanish Sign
       Language) | BSL = British Sign Language | E. ab.

843   Fenlon, Jordan; Schembri, Adam C.; Rentelis, Ramas; Vinson, David P.;
       Cormier, Kearsy: Using conversational data to determine lexical fre-
       quency in British Sign Language : the influence of text type. – *Lingua*
       143, 2014, 187-202.

844   Schermer, Trude: Lexicon. – (633), 173-195.

3.1.   LEXICOLOGY

845   Adone, Dany; Bauer, Anastasia; Cumberbatch, Keren; Maypilama,
       Elaine L. : Colour signs in two indigenous sign languages. – (1047),
       53-86.

846   Báez Montero, Inmaculada C.; Fernández Soneira, Ana: Colours and
       numerals in Spanish Sign Language (LSE). – (300), 73-121.

847   Bank, Richard; Crasborn, Onno A.; Hout, Roeland van: Variation in
       mouth actions with manual signs in Sign Language of the Netherlands
       (NGT). – *SLLing* 14/2, 2011, 248-270.

848   Battaglia, Katia; Cardinaletti, Anna; Cecchetto, Carlo; Donati,
       Caterina; Geraci, Carlo; Mereghetti, Emiliano: La variazione nel les-
       sico della Lingua dei Segni Italiana. – (12), 271-280.

849   Battaglia, Katia: Variazione lessicale e fonologica nella LIS. – (621),
       189-203.

850   Bianchini, Claudia S.; Di Renzo, Alessio; Lucioli, Tommaso; Rossini,
       Paolo; [Antinoro, Elena] Antinoro Pizzuto, Elena: Unità lessematiche

        e strutture di grande iconicità nella lingua dei segni italiana (LIS) : nuovi dati e nuove metodologie di analisi. – (12), 281-294.

851   Ebling, Sarah; Konrad, Reiner; Boyes Braem, Penny; Langer, Gabriele: Factors to consider when making lexical comparisons of sign languages : notes from an ongoing comparison of German Sign Language and Swiss German Sign Language. – *SLStud* 16/1, 2015, 30-56 | E. ab.

852   Engberg-Pedersen, Elisabeth: Expressions of causation in Danish Sign Language. – *SLLing* 13/1, 2010, 40-67.

853   Hendriks, Bernadet; Dufoe, Shelley: Non-native or native vocabulary in Mexican Sign Language. – *SLLing* 17/1, 2014, 20-55.

854   Hendriks, Bernadet: Kinship and colour terms in Mexican Sign Language. – (300), 333-349.

855   Hollman, Liivi: Colour terms, kinship terms and numerals in Estonian Sign Language. – (300), 41-72.

856   Hollman, Liivi: Miks *must* on MUST ja *valge* VALGE : eesti viipekeele värvinimedest. – *KjK* 61/11, 2008, 847-862 | E. ab.: Why black is MUST and white is VALGE : on colour terms in Estonian Sign Language.

857   Hollman, Liivi; Sutrop, Urmas: Basic color terms in Estonian Sign Language. – *SLStud* 11/2, 2010, 130-157.

858   Konrad, Reiner: The lexical structure of German Sign Language (DGS) in the light of empirical LSP lexicography : on how to integrate iconicity in a corpus-based lexicon model. – *SLLing* 16/1, 2013, 111-118 | Diss. ab.

859   Maxaroblidze, Tamar: drois sist'ema kartul žest'ur enaši. – *EnS* 2014 (2015), 209-218 | E. ab.: The temporal system in the Georgian Sign Language.

860   Maxaroblidze, Tamar: kartuli žest'uri enis leksik'is šesaxeb. – *IKE* 43, 2015, 116-143 | E. ab.: On Georgian Sign Language lexical level.

861   Palfreyman, Nick: Colour terms in Indonesian sign language varieties : a preliminary study. – (300), 269-299.

862   Richterová, Klára; Macurová, Alena; Nováková, Radka: Kinship terminology in Czech Sign Language. – (300), 163-207.

863   Rodrigues, Isabel Cristina; Baalbaki, Angela Corrêa Ferreira: Práticas sociais entre línguas em contato : os empréstimos linguísticos do português à Libras = Social practices between languages in contact : the loanwords from Portuguese to Brazilian Sign Language (Libras). – *RBLApl* 14/4, 2014, 1095-1120 | E. ab.

864   Stamp, Rose: Sociolinguistic variation, language change and contact in the British Sign Language (BSL) lexicon : (Deafness Cognition &

Language Research Centre, University College London, 2013). – *SLLing* 18/1, 2015, 158-166 | Diss. ab.

865 Sverrisdóttir, Rannveig; Þorvaldsdóttir, Kristín Lena: Why is the SKY BLUE? : on colour signs in Icelandic Sign Language. – (300), 209-249.

866 Taşçı, Süleyman S.; Göksel, Aslı: The morphological categorization of polymorphemic lexemes : a study based on lexicalized fingerspelled forms in TİD. – *DAD* 2, 2014, 165-180.

867 Vysuček, Petr: *Specifické znaky v českém znakovém jazyce.* – Praha : Česká komora tlumočníků znakového jazyka, 2008. – 53 p. | Specific signs in the Czech sign language.

3.2. LEXICOGRAPHY

868 Fenlon, Jordan; Cormier, Kearsy; Schembri, Adam C.: Building BSL SignBank : the lemma dilemma revisited. – *IJLex* 28/2, 2015, 169-206.

869 Kosiba, Olgierd; Grenda, Piotr: *Leksykon języka migowego.* – Bogatynia : Silentium, 2011. – 360 p. | Dictionary of Polish Sign Language.

870 Kristoffersen, Jette Hedegaard; Troelsgård, Thomas: En ordbog uden ord : lemmatiseringsproblemer i en tegnsprogsordbog. – *SpriN* 2010, 81-91 | A dictionary without words : lemmatisation problems in a Sign Language dictionary.

871 *Lesotho Sign Language learners' dictionary* / produced by National Association of the Deaf Lesotho (NADL), in association with Department of African Languages and Literatures (NUL) ; compiled by 'Malillo E. M. Machobane and Litšepiso Matlosa ; illustrations and layout by Peter Maphatšoe. – S. l. : S. n., 2010. – 302 p.

872 Linde-Usiekniewicz, Jadwiga; Czajkowski-Kisil, Małgorzata; Łacheta, Joanna: Między leksykografią opisową a przekładową : Słownik polskiego języka migowego (PJM). – *PF* 68, 2016, 225-244 | Between monolingual and bilingual lexicography : the *Dictionary of Polish sign language* (PJM) | E. ab.

873 Schmaling, Constanze H.: Dictionaries of African sign languages : an overview. – *SLStud* 12/2, 2012, 236-278 | E. ab | Erratum cf. *Sign language studies* 13/1 2012, p. 145.

874 Thamm, Ulrike: *Wörterbücher der Deutschen Gebärdensprache : sprachspezifische Besonderheiten und deren Bearbeitung in ausgewählten Wörterbüchern.* – Frankfurt am Main : Lang, 2014. – 231 p. – (Leipziger Studien zur angewandten Linguistik und Translatologie ; 14).

875   Wallang, Melissa G.: The making of the Shillong Sign Language
       Multimedia Lexicon (ShSL MML). – *SLStud* 15/3, 2015, 296-321 | E. ab.

3.2.2.   PLURILINGUAL LEXICOGRAPHY

876   Cabeza Pereiro, Carmen: En busca de la precisión : análisis de una
       configuración manual en el *Diccionario normativo de la lengua de sig-
       nos española.* – (43), 167-181.

877   [Fourie, Hanelle] Fourie Blair, Hanelle: Ekwivalentverhoudings in
       tweetalige woordeboeke : implikasies vir die databasis van 'n elek-
       troniese tweetalige woordeboek van Suid-Afrikaanse Gebaretaal en
       Afrikaans. – *Lexikos* 25, 2015, 151-169 | Equivalent relations in bilingual
       dictionaries : implications for the database of an electronic bilin-
       gual dictionary of South African Sign Language AND Afrikaans | E. &
       Afrikaans ab.

878   Fourie, Hanelle: *'n Leksikografiese model vir 'n elektroniese tweet-
       alige grondslagfasewoordeboek van Suid-Afrikaanse Gebaretaal en
       Afrikaans.* – Stellenbosch : Universiteit van Stellenbosch, 2013. – [16],
       446 p. | [Lexicographical model for an electronic bilingual diction-
       ary of South African Sign Language and Afrikaans] | Diss. at Univ. of
       Stellenbosch, March 2013 | E. & Afrikaans ab.

879   Hollak, Józef; Jagodziński, Teofil: *Słownik mimiczny dla głuchoniemych
       i osób z nimi styczność mających.* – Łódź : Polski Związek Głuchych
       Oddział Łódzki, 2011. – 512 p. | Repr. of the 1879 ed | Józef Hollak (1812-
       1890) ; Teofil Jagodziński (1833-1907).

880   McKee, Rachel M. Locker; McKee, David: Making an online diction-
       ary of New Zealand Sign Language. – *Lexikos* 23, 2013, 500-531 | E. &
       Afrikaans ab.

3.3.   ETYMOLOGY

881   Ferrerons, Ramon: *Primer diccionari general i etimològic de la llengua
       de signes catalana.* 2 vols. – Barcelona : Documenta universitaria,
       2011. – 506; 510 p.

3.4.   TERMINOLOGY

882   Geer, Leah C.: Kinship in Mongolian Sign Language. – *SLStud* 11/4,
       2011, 594-605 | E. ab.

883   Oliveira, Janine Soares; Weininger, Markus Johannes: Densidade de
       informação, complexidade fonológica e suas implicações para a orga-
       nização de glossários de termos técnicos da língua de sinais brasileira.
       – CdT 2 (32), 2013, 141-163 | Information density, phonological com-
       plexity and its implications for the organization of glossaries of tech-
       nical terms in Brazilian Sign Language.

4.   SEMANTICS AND PRAGMATICS

884   Nilsson, Anna-Lena: Embodying metaphors : signed language inter-
       preters at work. – CognL 27/1, 2016, 35-65.

4.1.   SEMANTICS

885   Arık, Engin: Türk İşaret Dili'nde mekânsal dil. – (615), 315-335 | Spatial
       relations in Turkish Sign Language.
886   Bos, Heleen F.: An analysis of main verb agreement and auxiliary
       agreement in NGT within the theory of Conceptual Semantics
       (Jackendoff 1990). – SLLing 20/2, 2017, 228-252 | Preface (p. 221-227)
       and afterword (p. 253-269) | Commentary cf. 887.
887   Gökgöz, Kadir: Commentary on Bos (1998). – SLLing 20/2, 2017, 270-
       278 | Commentary on 886.
888   Hwang, So-One K.; Tomita, Nozomi; Morgan, Hope E.; Ergin, Rabia;
       İlkbaşaran, Deniz; Seegers, Sharon; Lepic, Ryan; Padden, Carol A.: Of
       the body and the hands : patterned iconicity for semantic categories.
       – LCog 9/4, 2017, 573-602 | E. ab.
889   Kimmel'man, Vadim I.; Kyuseva, Maria; Lomakina, Yana; Perova,
       Daria: On the notion of metaphor in sign languages : some observa-
       tions based on Russian Sign Language. – SLLing 20/2, 2017, 157-182 |
       E. ab.
890   Napoli, Donna Jo; Sutton-Spence, Rachel L.; Müller de Quadros,
       Ronice: Influence of predicate sense on word order in sign languages :
       intensional and extensional verbs. – Language 93/3, 2017, 641-670 |
       E. ab.
891   Özyürek, Aslı; Perniss, Pamela M.: Event representation in signed
       languages. – (107), 84-107 | A contrastive analysis of Turkish Sign
       Language & German Sign Language.
892   Perniss, Pamela M.; Zwitserlood, Inge; Özyürek, Aslı: Does space
       structure spatial language? : a comparison of spatial expression across
       sign languages. – Language 91/3, 2015, 611-641.

893   Pfau, Roland; Steinbach, Markus: Modality and meaning : plural-
       ity of relations in German Sign Language. – *Lingua* 170, 2016, 69-91 |
       E. ab.

894   Risler, Annie: Expression du déplacement dans les langues signées :
       comment parler d'espace dans une langue spatiale? – *Faits* 42,
       2013, 217-244 | Fr. & E. ab.: Motion events encoding in French Sign
       Language : expression of spatial events in a language based on spatial
       relations.

895   Schlenker, Philippe: Anaphora : insights from sign language (sum-
       mary). – (8), 83-107.

896   Schlenker, Philippe; Lamberton, Jonathan; Santoro, Mirko: Iconic
       variables. – *L&P* 36/2, 2013, 91-149.

897   Selvik, Kari-Anne: Tidsuttrykk i rommet : en kognitiv lingvistisk
       tilnærming til en gruppe tidsuttrykk i norsk tegnspråk. – *NLT* 29/1,
       2011, 38-53 | Expressing time in space : a cognitive linguistic approach
       to a group of temporal expressions in Norwegian Sign Language |
       E. ab.

898   Šůchová, Lucie: Metafory w czeskim języku migowym. – (196), 131-150
       | Metaphors in Czech sign lg.E. ab.

899   Šůchová, Lucie: Znakové jazyky a kognitivní lingvistika : problema-
       tika konceptuálních metafor. – *JazA* 48/1-2, 2011, 5-15 | Sign languages
       and cognitive linguistics : the question of conceptual metaphors |
       Cz. ab.

900   Vintar, Špela: Lexical properties of Slovene Sign Language : a corpus-
       based study. – *SLStud* 15/2, 2015, 182-201 | E. ab.

901   Wilbur, Ronnie B.: The semantics-phonology interface. – (218),
       355-380.

4.1.1.   LEXICAL SEMANTICS

902   Kosecki, Krzysztof: Metaphorical aspects of selected signs in Polish
       sign language. – *LSil* 29, 2008, 67-74 | E. ab.

903   Oomen, Marloes: Iconicity in argument structure : psych-verbs in Sign
       Language of the Netherlands. – *SLLing* 20/1, 2017, 55-108 | E. ab.

904   Takkinen, Ritva; Jantunen, Tommi; Seilola, Irja: A typological look at
       kinship terms, colour terms and numbers in Finnish Sign Language. –
       (300), 123-162.

905   [Zucchi, Alessandro] Zucchi, Sandro: Along the time line : tense and
       time adverbs in Italian Sign Language. – *NLS* 17/2, 2009, 99-139.

4.1.2. GRAMMATICAL SEMANTICS

906 Barberà Altimira, Gemma: *The meaning of space in sign language : reference, specificity and structure in Catalan Sign Language discourse.* – Berlin : De Gruyter Mouton ; Preston, UK : Ishara Press, 2015. – xix, 271 p. – (Sign languages and deaf communities ; 4).

907 Barberà, Gemma: Indefiniteness and specificity marking in Catalan Sign Language (LSC). – *SLLing* 19/1, 2016, 1-36.

908 Barberà, Gemma; Quer, Josep: Impersonal reference in Catalan Sign Language (LSC). – (217), 237-258.

909 Beuzeville, Louise de; Johnston, Trevor; Schembri, Adam C.: The use of space with indicating verbs in Auslan : a corpus-based investigation. – *SLLing* 12/1, 2009, 53-82.

910 Bolgueroni, Thais; Viotti, Evani: Referência nominal em língua de sinais brasileira (libras). – *TAL-RLL* 15/1, 2013, 15-50 | E. ab.

911 Coppola, Marie; Senghas, Ann: Deixis in an emerging sign language. – (218), 543-569.

912 Dikyuva, Hasan: Türk İşaret Dili'nde görünüş kodlayan el-dışı işaretler. – (615), 297-314 | [Non-manual signs to mark aspect in Turkish Sign Language].

913 Herrmann, Annika; Steinbach, Markus: Quotation in sign languages : a visible context shift. – (112), 203-228.

914 Horton, L.; Goldin-Meadow, Susan; Coppola, Marie; Senghas, Ann; Brentari, Diane K.: Forging a morphological system out of two dimensions : agentivity and number. – *OpLi* 1/1, 2015, 596-613 | Electronic publ.

915 Meir, Irit; Padden, Carol A.; Aronoff, Mark; Sandler, Wendy: Competing iconicities in the structure of languages. – *CognL* 24/2, 2013, 309-343 | E. ab.

916 Özyürek, Aslı; Zwitserlood, Inge; Perniss, Pamela M.: Locative expressions in signed languages : a view from Turkish Sign Language (TİD). – *Linguistics* 48/5, 2010, 1111-1145.

917 Padden, Carol A.; Meir, Irit; Aronoff, Mark; Sandler, Wendy: The grammar of space in two new sign languages. – (218), 570-592.

918 Perniss, Pamela M.: Space and iconicity in German Sign Language (DGS). – *SLLing* 11/1, 2008, 123-129 | Ab. of the author's Radboud University, Nijmegen, 2007 diss.

919 Sinte, Aurélie: Expression of time in French Belgian Sign Language (LSFB). – (217), 205-236.

920   Sinte, Aurélie: Français – Langue des signes française de Belgique
      (LSFB) : quelques éléments d'analyse contrastive des temps verbaux.
      – CAFLS 16/1, 2010, 129-152.

921   Slowikowska Schrøder, Bogumila: Imperativ i norsk tegnspråk. – NLT
      29/1, 2011, 136-157 | The imperative in Norwegian Sign Language | E. ab.

922   Šůchová, Lucie: Konceptualizace buducnosti a minulosti v českém
      znakovém jazyce a v polském znakovém jazyce. – (1), 145-160 |
      Conceptualization of the future and the past in Czech and Polish sign
      lgs. | Pol. & G. ab.

923   Xavier, André Nogueira; Wilcox, Sherman E.: Necessity and possibility
      modals in Brazilian Sign Language (Libras). – LT 18/3, 2014, 449-488.

924   Zwitserlood, Inge; Perniss, Pamela M.; Özyürek, Aslı: An empiri-
      cal investigation of expression of multiple entities in Turkish Sign
      Language (TİD) : considering the effects of modality. – Lingua 122/14,
      2012, 1636-1667

4.2. PRAGMATICS, DISCOURSE ANALYSIS AND TEXT GRAMMAR

925   Baker, Anne Edith; Bogaerde, Beppie van den: Interaction and dis-
      course. – (633), 73-91.

926   Barberà, Gemma: The meaning of space in Catalan Sign Language
      (LSC) : reference, specificity and structure in signed discourse. –
      SLLing 16/1, 2013, 97-105 | Diss. ab.

927   Barberà, Gemma: Use and functions of spatial planes in Catalan Sign
      Language (LSC) discourse. – SLStud 14/2, 2014, 147-174 | E. ab.

928   Bōnō, Mayumi: Shuwa sansha kaiwa ni okeru shintai to shisen. –
      Nihongogaku 32/1, 2013, 46-55 | [Body and eye movement in sign lan-
      guage conversation in three persons].

929   Cibulka, Paul: On how to do things with holds : manual movement
      phases as part of interactional practices in signed conversation. –
      SLStud 16/4, 2016, 447-472 | E. ab.

930   Cormier, Kearsy; Smith, Sandra; [Sevcikova, Zed] Sevcikova-Sehyr,
      Zed: Rethinking constructed action. – SLLing 18/2, 2015, 167-204.

931   Cormier, Kearsy; Smith, Sandra; Zwets, Martine: Framing constructed
      action in British Sign Language narratives. – JoP 55, 2013, 119-139.

932   Engberg-Pedersen, Elisabeth: Perspective in signed discourse : the
      privileged status of the signer's locus and gaze. – OpLi 1/1, 2015, 411-431
      | Electronic. publ.

933   Engberg-Pedersen, Elisabeth: Tilegnelse af fortællerperspektiv og ref-
      erentperspektiv i dansk tegnsprog : introduktion af en ny referent. –

NySS 48, 2015, 9-35 | E. ab.: Acquisition of narrator perspective and referent perspective in Danish Sign Language : introducing a new referent in a narrative | E. ab.

934   Fehrmann, Gisela: Exploiting space in German Sign Language : linguistic and topographic reference in signed discourse. – (31), 607-636 | Cf. comm. by Holger Diessel, p. 687-692.

935   Fischer, Renate; Kollien, Simon: Pejorative aspects attributed to hearing people in signed constructed dialogue. – (105), 325-353.

936   Floyd, Simeon; Manrique, Elizabeth; Rossi, Giovanni; Torreira, Francisco: Timing of visual bodily behavior in repair sequences : evidence from three languages. – *DP* 53/3, 2016, 175-204 | E. ab.

937   Fuks, Orit: Gradient and categorically : handshape's two semiotic dimensions in Israeli Sign Language discourse. – *JoP* 60, 2014, 207-225.

938   George, Johnny: Universals in the visual-kinesthetic modality : politeness marking features in Japanese Sign Language (JSL). – (17), 129-143.

939   Groeber, Simone; Pochon-Berger, Evelyne: Turns and turn-taking in sign language interaction : a study of turn-final holds. – *JoP* 65, 2014, 121-136.

940   Halvorsen, Rolf Piene; Amundsen, Guri: Noen diskursmarkører i norsk tegnspråk. – *NLT* 29/1, 2011, 117-135 | Some discourse markers in Norwegian Sign Language | E. ab.

941   Hansen, Martje; Heßmann, Jens: Researching linguistic features of text genres in a DGS corpus : the case of finger loci. – *SLLing* 18/1, 2015, 1-40.

942   Haviland, John B.: *Xi to vi*: "Over that way, look!" : (meta)spatial representation in an emerging (Mayan?) sign language. – (31), 334-400 | Also on the use of gestures in spoken Tzotzil | Cf. comm. by Anja Stukenbrock, p. 401-408.

943   Herrmann, Annika: The marking of information structure in German Sign Language. – *Lingua* 165/B, 2015, 277-297.

944   Herrmann, Annika: *Modal and focus particles in sign languages : a cross-linguistic study.* – Berlin : De Gruyter Mouton ; Nijmegen : Ishara Press, 2013. – xix, 400 p. – (Sign languages and deaf communities ; 2) | On German Sign Language, Sign Language of the Netherlands, and Irish Sign Language.

945   Hoetjes, Marieke; Krahmer, Emiel; Swerts, Marc: Do repeated references result in sign reduction? – *SLLing* 17/1, 2014, 56-81.

946   Jarque, Maria Josep; Pascual, Esther: Mixed viewpoints in factual and fictive discourse in Catalan Sign Language narratives. – (127), 259-280 | E. ab.

947 Kelepir, Meltem; Göksel, Aslı: Türk İşaret Dili'nde aktarılmış anlatımın özellikleri. – (615), 337-360 | [Aspects of reported utterances in Turkish Sign Language].

948 Kikuchi, Kōhei; Bōnō, Mayumi: Sōgo kōi toshite no shuwa tsūyaku katsudō : tsūyakusha o kaishita junban kaishi no tame no kikite kakutoku tetsuzuki no bunseki. – *NinK* 22/1, 2015, 167-180 | Sign interpreting as an interaction : an analysis on procedures of getting addressee for turn-opening mediated by sign interpreters | E. ab.

949 Kikuchi, Kōhei: Nihon shuwa kaiwa ni okeru tān teikingu mekanizumu : rinsetsu ōtō pea to sono shigunaru no bunseki. – *ShK* 17, 2008, 29-45 | [Turn taking mechanism in Japan Sign Language : analysis of adjacency pairs and their signs].

950 Kimmel'man, Vadim I.: Information structure in Russian Sign Language and Sign Language of the Netherlands : (University of Amsterdam, 2014). – *SLLing* 18/1, 2015, 142-150 | Diss. ab.

951 Kimmel'man, Vadim I.; Vink, Lianne: Question-answer pairs in Sign Language of the Netherlands. – *SLStud* 17/4, 2017, 417-449 | E. ab.

952 Lackner, Andrea: *Functions of head and body movements in Austrian Sign Language.* – Berlin : De Gruyter Mouton ; Preston, UK : Ishara Press, 2017. – xxiv, 261 p. – (Sign languages and deaf communities ; 9).

953 Leite, Tarcísio de Arantes; McCleary, Leland: A identificação de unidades gramaticais na libras : uma proposta de abordagem baseada-no-uso. – *TAL-RLL* 15/1, 2013, 62-87 | Identifying grammatical units in Libras : a proposal for a usage-based approach | E. ab | Libras = Brazilian Sign Language.

954 Makaroğlu, Bahtiyar: Türk İşaret Dili'nde soru tümcelerinin görünümü : kaş hareketlerinin rolü. – (615), 233-252 | [Interrogatives in Turkish Sign Language : the role of eyebrow movements].

955 Manrique, Elizabeth: Other-initiated repair in Argentine Sign Language. – *OpLi* 2/1, 2016, 1-34 | E. ab.

956 Mapson, Rachel: Polite appearances : how non-manual features convey politeness in British Sign Language. – *JPLR* 10/2, 2014, 157-184 | E. ab.

957 Matsuoka, Kazumi; Gajewski, Jon: The polarity-sensitive intensifier mouth gestures in Japanese Sign Language. – *JJLing* 29, 2013, 31-49 | E. ab.

958 McKee, Rachel M. Locker; Wallingford, Sophia: 'So, well, whatever': discourse functions of palm-up in New Zealand Sign Language. – *SLLing* 14/2, 2011, 213-247.

959   Meurant, Laurence: Role shift, anaphora and discourse polyphony in
      Sign Language of Southern Belgium (LSFB). – (30), 319-352.

960   Morales López, Esperanza; Reigosa Varela, César; Bobillo García,
      Nancy: Word order and informative functions (topic and focus) in
      Spanish Signed Language utterances. – *JoP* 44/4, 2012, 474-489.

961   Morgan, Michael W.: Participant tracking in Nepali Sign Language
      narrative. – *NepL* 28, 2013, 86-93.

962   Perniss, Pamela M.; Özyürek, Aslı: Representations of action, motion,
      and location in sign space : a comparison of German (DGS) and
      Turkish (TİD) Sign Language narratives. – (30), 353-377.

963   Siyavoshi, Sara: The role of the non-dominant hand in ZEI discourse
      structure. – *SLStud* 18/1, 2017, 58-72 | E. ab.

964   Sutton-Spence, Rachel L.; Napoli, Donna Jo: Anthropomorphism
      in sign languages : a look at poetry and storytelling with a focus on
      British Sign Language. – *SLStud* 10/4, 2010, 442-475.

965   Sze, Felix Yim Binh: Is Hong Kong Sign Language a topic-prominent
      language? – *Linguistics* 53/4, 2015, 809-876.

966   Sze, Felix Yim Binh: Right dislocated pronominals in Hong Kong Sign
      Language. – *JoP* 44/14, 2012, 1949-1965.

967   Thompson, Robin L.; England, Rachel; Woll, Bencie; Lu, Jenny;
      Mumford, Katherine; Morgan, Gary: Deaf and hearing children's pic-
      ture naming : impact of age of acquisition and language modality on
      representational gesture. – *LIA* 8/1, 2017, 69-88 | E. & Fr. ab.

968   Yasugahira, Yūta; Horiuchi, Yasuo; Nishida, Masafumi; Kuroiwa,
      Shingo: Nihon shuwa no shuwa hatsuwa sokudo no chigai ni yoru
      te dōsa henka no bunseki. – *ShK* 17, 2008, 57-68 | [Hand movement
      change caused by the difference in speed of sign utterances in Japan
      Sign Language].

5. STYLISTICS

969   Kaneko, Michiko; Mesch, Johanna: Eye gaze in creative sign language.
      – *SLStud* 13/3, 2013, 372-400 | E. ab.

7. TRANSLATION

970   Albres, Neiva Aquino; Lacerda, Cristina Broglia Feitosa de:
      Interpretação educacional como campo de pesquisa : estudo bib-
      liométrico de publicações internacionais e suas marcas no campo

nacional. – *CdT* 1 (31), 2013, 179-204 | Educational interpreting as a field of research.

971   [Antinoro, Elena] Antinoro Pizzuto, Elena; Chiari, Isabella; Rossini, Paolo: Strumenti per la traduzione della Lingua dei Segni Italiana : critiche e proposte per una ricerca responsabile. – (14), 159-172.

972   Danese, Lisa; Bertone, Carmela; De Souza Faria, Carla Valeria: La traduzione dall'italiano alla Lingua dei Segni Italiana (LIS) : nuove prospettive dì ricerca. – (14), 223-228.

973   Danese, Lisa: La traduzione dall'italiano alla LIS : proposta di accessibilità dei contenuti turistici e culturali. – (621), 237-251.

974   Fontana, Sabina; Zuccalà, Amir: Traduzione e identità : impatto sociolinguistico dell'interpretariato da e verso la lingua dei segni nella percezione dell'identità comunitaria sorda. – (14), 173-188.

975   Gianfreda, Gabriele; Di Renzo, Alessio: Conversazioni in Lingua dei Segni Italiana (LIS) : rappresentazione e traducibilità linguistica. – (14), 207-222.

8.   SCRIPT, ORTHOGRAPHY

976   Maxaroblidze, Tamar: kartuli dakt'iluri anbani. – *IKE* 42, 2014, 144-165 | E. ab.: The Georgian dactyl alphabet.

9.1.   ORIGIN OF LANGUAGE

977   Senghas, Ann; Özyürek, Aslı; Goldin-Meadow, Susan: Homesign as a way-station between co-speech gesture and sign language : the evolution of segmenting and sequencing. – (117), 62-76 | Exemplified by Nicaraguan Sign Language.

9.2.   PSYCHOLINGUISTICS

978   Bogaerde, Beppie van den; Buré, Marjolein; Fortgens, Connie: Bilingualism and deaf education. – (633), 325-336.

979   Cáo, Yǔ; Lǐ, Héng: Eryǔ shuǐpíng hé èryǔ tōngdào duì shuāngyǔzhě zhùyì kòngzhì nénglì de yǐngxiǎng. – *XDW* 39/3, 2016, 390-398 | The influence of L2 proficiency and modality on bilinguals' attention control ability | Chin. & E. ab.

980   Efthimiou, Eleni: Processing cumulative morphology information in GSL : the case of pronominal reference in a three-dimensional morphological system. – (38), 114-128 | Gr. ab | GSL = Greek Sign Language.

981   Massone, María Ignacia; Baez, Mónica: Deaf children's construction
       of writing. – *SLStud* 9/4, 2009, 457-479.

982   Schermer, Trude; Pfau, Roland: Psycholinguistics. – (633), 25-50.

983   Takashima, Yufuko: Nihon shuwa no shinri gengogakuteki chōsa no
       jissen to mondai. – *NinK* 22/1, 2015, 181-193 | Some issues on psycholin-
       guistic investigation of Japanese sign language | E. ab.

984   Villameriel, Saúl; Dias, Patricia; Costello, Brendan; Carreiras, Manuel,
       orcid.org/0000-0001-6726-7613: Cross-language and cross-modal
       activation in hearing bimodal bilinguals. – *JM&L* 87, 2016, 59-70 |
       E. ab.

985   Vinson, David P.; Thompson, Robin L.; Skinner, Robert; Vigliocco,
       Gabriella: A faster path between meaning and form? : iconicity facili-
       tates sign recognition and production in British Sign Language. –
       JM&L 82, 2015, 56-85.

9.2.1.   LANGUAGE PRODUCTION

986   Baus, Cristina; Gutiérrez-Sigut, Eva; Quer, Josep; Carreiras, Manuel,
       orcid.org/0000-0001-6726-7613: Lexical access in Catalan Signed
       Language (LSC) production. – *Cognition* 108/3, 2008.

987   Branchini, Chiara; Donati, Caterina: Assessing lexicalism through
       bimodal eyes. – *Glossa* 1/1, 2016, 48 | E. ab.

988   Carreiras, Manuel, orcid.org/0000-0001-6726-7613; Gutiérrez-Sigut,
       Eva; Baquero, Silvia; Corina, David P.: Lexical processing in Spanish
       Sign Language (LSE). – *JM&L* 58/1, 2008, 100-122.

989   Goldin-Meadow, Susan; Brentari, Diane K.; Coppola, Marie; Horton,
       L.; Senghas, Ann: Watching language grow in the manual modal-
       ity : nominals, predicates, and handshapes. – *Cognition* 136, 2015,
       381-395.

990   Gutiérrez-Sigut, Eva; Payne, Heather; MacSweeney, Mairéad:
       Examining the contribution of motor movement and language domi-
       nance to increased left lateralization during sign generation in native
       signers. – *B&L* 159, 2016, 109-117 | E. ab.

991   Kaufmann, Emily; Philipp, Andrea M.: Language-switch costs and
       dual-response costs in bimodal bilingual language production. –
       Bilingualism 20/2, 2017, 418-434 | E. ab.

992   Vletsi, Eleni; Hrisovalantou Liapi, Irene; Stavrakaki, Stavroula;
       Marshall, Chloë R.; Grouios, George: Assessing verbal fluency in Greek
       Sign Language. – (26), 612-619.

993   Holt, Gineke ten; Doorn, Arna van; Ridder, Huib de; Reinders, M. J. T.;
      Hendriks, E. A.: Which fragments of a sign enable its recognition? –
      SLStud 9/2, 2009, 211-239.

994   Holt, Gineke ten; Doorn, Arna van; Ridder, Huib de; Reinders, M. J. T.;
      Hendriks, E. A.: Signs in which handshape and hand orientation are
      either not visible or are only partially visible : what is the consequence
      for lexical recognition? – *SLStud* 10/1, 2009, 5-35.

995   Marshall, Chloë R.; Rowley, Katherine; Atkinson, Joanna: Modality-
      dependent and -independent factors in the organisation of the signed
      language lexicon : insights from semantic and phonological fluency
      tasks in BSL. – *JPR* 43/5, 2014, 587-610 | E. ab.

996   Ortega, Gerardo; Morgan, Gary: The effect of iconicity in the mental
      lexicon of hearing non-signers and proficient signers : evidence of
      cross-modal priming. – *LCN* 30/5, 2015, 574-585.

997   [Sevcikova, Zed] Sevcikova-Sehyr, Zed; Cormier, Kearsy: Perceptual
      categorization of handling handshapes in British Sign Language. –
      LCog 8/4, 2016, 501-532 | E. ab.

998   Kubus, Okan; Villwock, Agnes; Morford, Jill P.; Rathmann, Christian:
      Word recognition in deaf readers : cross-language activation of
      German Sign Language and German. – *AP* 36/4, 2015, 831-854.

999   Baker, Anne Edith; Bogaerde, Beppie van den; Jansma, Sonja:
      Acquisition. – (633), 51-72.

1000 Beijsterveldt, Liesbeth M. van; Hell, Janet G. van: Lexical noun phrases
      in texts written by deaf children and adults with different proficiency
      levels in sign language. – *IJBEB* 13/4, 2010, 439-468.

1001 Dakwa, Francis Emson; Musengi, Martin: A look at language problems
      experienced by children with hearing impairments : the learner's
      experience. – *SAfrJAL* 35/2, 2015, 177-180.

1002 *Handbook of Japanese applied linguistics* / Ed. by Masahiko Minami. –
      Berlin : De Gruyter Mouton, 2016. – xliii, 535 p. – (Handbooks of
      Japanese language and linguistics ; 10) | Not analyzed.

9.3.1.   FIRST LANGUAGE ACQUISITION, CHILD LANGUAGE

1003   [Chen, Deborah] Chen Pichler, Deborah; Hochgesang, Julie A.; Lillo-
        Martin, Diane C.; Müller de Quadros, Ronice; Reynolds, Wanette: Best
        practices for building a bimodal/bilingual child language corpus. –
        SLStud 16/3, 2016, 361-388 | E. ab.
1004   Sümer, Beyza: Scene-setting and referent introduction in sign and
        spoken languages : what does modality tell us?. – (198), 193-220 |
        E. ab.
1005   Sümer, Beyza; Zwitserlood, Inge; Perniss, Pamela M.; Özyürek, Aslı:
        Yer bildiren ifadelerin Türkçe ve Türk İşaret Dili'nde (TİD) çocuklar
        tarafından edinimi. – (615), 157-182 | [The acquisiton of spatial expres-
        sions by children in Turkish and Turkish Sign Language].

9.3.1.1.   FIRST LANGUAGE ACQUISITION BY PRE-SCHOOL CHILDREN

1006   Blondel, Marion; Boutet, Dominique; Beaupoil-Hourdel, Pauline;
        Morgenstern, Aliyah: La négation chez les enfants signeurs et non
        signeurs : des patrons gestuels communs. – *LIA* 8/1, 2017, 141-171 |
        [Negation in signing and non-signing children : common gestural pat-
        terns] | E. & Fr. ab.
1007   Caët, Stéphanie; Limousin, Fanny; Morgenstern, Aliyah: A functional
        approach to self-points and self-reference in a deaf signing child and
        the (dis)continuity issue in child language. – *LIA* 8/1, 2017, 117-140 |
        E. & Fr. ab.
1008   Carmo, Patrícia do; Mineiro, Ana; Castelo Branco, Joana; Müller de
        Quadros, Ronice; Castro-Caldas, Alexandre: Handshape is the hard-
        est path in Portuguese Sign Language acquisition : towards a universal
        modality constraint. – *SLLing* 16/1, 2013, 75-90.
1009   Cormier, Kearsy; Schembri, Adam C.; Vinson, David P.; Orfanidou,
        Eleni: First language acquisition differs from second language acqui-
        sition in prelingually deaf signers : evidence from sensitivity to gram-
        maticality judgement in British Sign Language. – *Cognition* 124/1, 2012,
        50-65.
1010   Cramér-Wolrath, Emelie: Mediating native Swedish Sign Language :
        first language in gestural modality interactions at storytime. – *SLStud*
        15/3, 2015, 266-295 | E. ab.
1011   Fridman Mintz, Boris: De sordos hablantes, semilingües y señantes. –
        LynX 8, 2009, 93-126.

1012   Hatzopoulou, Marianna: Acquisition of reference to self and others in
        Greek Sign Language (Stockholm University, 2008). – *SLLing* 13/1, 2010,
        83-91 | Abstract of the author's doctoral diss.

1013   Limousin, Fanny; Blondel, Marion: Prosodie et acquisition de la
        langue des signes française : acquisition monolingue LSF et bilingue
        LSG-français. – *LIA* 1/1, 2010, 82-109 | E. ab.

1014   Marshall, Chloë R.; Rowley, Katherine; Mason, Kathryn; Herman,
        Rosalind; Morgan, Gary: Lexical organization in deaf children who
        use British Sign Language : evidence from a semantic fluency task. –
        JChL 40/1, 2013, 193-220.

1015   Morgenstern, Aliyah; Beaupoil-Hourdel, Pauline; Blondel, Marion;
        Boutet, Dominique: A multimodal approach to the development of
        negation in signed and spoken languages : four case studies. – (146),
        15-36 | E. ab.

1016   Morgenstern, Aliyah; Caët, Stéphanie; Limousin, Fanny: Pointing and
        self-reference in French and French Sign Language. – *OpLi* 2/1, 2016,
        47-66 | E. ab.

1017   Ortega, Gerardo; Morgan, Gary: Comparing child and adult devel-
        opment of a visual phonological system. – *LIA* 1/1, 2010, 67-81 |
        Fr. ab.

1018   Slowikowska, Beata: Tidlig språkutvikling hos et døvt barn av døve
        foreldre. – *NLT* 29/1, 2011, 158-187 | Early language development in a
        deaf child of deaf parents | E. ab.

1019   Tomaszewski, Piotr: Interactions of deaf preschoolers : a comparison
        of the communicative behaviors of deaf children of deaf parents and
        of deaf children of hearing parents. – *PsychLC* 12/2, 2008, 69-87.

1020   Vos, Connie de: The Kata Kolok perfective in child signing : coordina-
        tion of manual and non-manual components. – (1047), 127-152.

9.3.1.2.   FIRST LANGUAGE ACQUISITION BY SCHOOL CHILDREN

1021   Becker, Claudia: Narrative competences of deaf children in German
        Sign Language. – *SLLing* 12/2, 2009, 113-160.

1022   Sallandre, Marie-Anne; Courtin, Cyril; Fusellier-Souza, Ivani;
        L'Huillier, Marie Thérèse: L'expression des déplacements chez l'enfant
        sourd en langue des signes française. – *LIA* 1/1, 2010, 41-66 | E. ab.

1023   Smith, Sandra; Cormier, Kearsy: In or out? : spatial scale and enact-
        ment in narratives of native and nonnative signing deaf children
        acquiring British Sign Language. – *SLStud* 14/3, 2014, 275-301 | E. ab.

1024   Sümer, Beyza; Perniss, Pamela M.; Özyürek, Aslı: A first study on the development of spatial viewpoint in sign language acquisition : the case of Turkish Sign Language. – (37), 223-240 | E. ab.

1025   Tomasuolo, Elena; Fellini, Laura; Di Renzo, Alessio; Volterra, Virginia: Assessing lexical production in deaf signing children with the Boston naming test. – *LIA* 1/1, 2010, 110-128 | Fr. ab.

9.3.1.3.   PLURILINGUAL LANGUAGE ACQUISITION

1026   Blondel, Marion; Tuller, Laurice: Pointing in bimodal, bilingual acquisition : a longitudinal study of a LSF-French bilingual child. – (30), 275-292.

1027   Cramér-Wolrath, Emelie: Parallel bimodal bilingual acquisition : a hearing child mediated in a deaf family. – *SLStud* 13/4, 2013, 516-540 | E. ab.

1028   Fung, Cat H.-M.; Tang, Gladys: Code-blending of functional heads in Hong Kong Sign Language and Cantonese : a case study. – *Bilingualism* 19/4, 2016, 754-781.

1029   Plaza Pust, Carolina: *Bilingualism and deafness : on language contact in the bilingual acquisition of sign language and written language.* – Berlin : De Gruyter Mouton ; Preston, UK : Ishara Press, 2016. – xxiv, 498 p. – (Sign languages and deaf communities ; 7).

1030   Rinaldi, Pasquale; Caselli, Maria Cristina: Language development in a bimodal bilingual child with cochlear implant : a longitudinal study. – *Bilingualism* 17/4, 2014, 798-809.

1031   Taira, Eiji: Mōdosuitchi ni okeru gengo kōzō no kirikae : bairingaru chōji K no kēsusutadī wo tōshite. – *ShK* 24, 2016, 31-49 | Switching language structure during mode-switches : the case study of the bilingual hearing child K | E. ab.

9.3.2.   SECOND LANGUAGE ACQUISITION

1032   Bel, Aurora; Ortells, Marta; Morgan, Gary: Reference control in the narratives of adult sign language learners. – *IJB* 19/5, 2015, 608-624.

1033   Ferrara, Lindsay; Nilsson, Anna-Lena: Describing spatial layouts as an L2M2 signed language learner. – *SLLing* 20/1, 2017, 1-26 | E. ab.

1034   Harrison, Simon: Visible bodily action in disfluencies when learning to sign : a classroom study of non-native sign language. – *TAL-RLL* 15/1, 2013, 51-61 | E. ab.

1035   Ortega, Gerardo: Acquisition of a signed phonological system by
        hearing adults : the role of sign structure and iconicity (Deafness,
        Cognition and Language Research Centre (DCAL), University College
        London (UCL), 2013). – *SLLing* 17/2, 2014, 267-275 | Diss. ab.

9.3.2.2.   GUIDED SECOND LANGUAGE ACQUISITION

1036   Ardito, Barbara; Caselli, Maria Cristina; Vecchietti, Angela; Volterra,
        Virginia: Deaf and hearing children : reading together in preschool. –
        (412), 137-164.

1037   Matsuoka, Kazumi; Lillo-Martin, Diane C.: Interpretation of bound
        pronouns by learners of Japanese Sign Language. – (39), 107-126 |
        E. ab.

1038   Ortega, Gerardo; Morgan, Gary: Phonological development in hear-
        ing learners of a sign language : the influence of phonological param-
        eters, sign complexity, and iconicity. – *LL* 65/3, 2015, 660-688.

1039   Plaza Pust, Carolina: Why variation matters : on language contact in
        the development of L2 written German. – (412), 73-135.

9.4.1.   NEUROLINGUISTICS

1040   Gutiérrez-Sigut, Eva; Daws, Richard; Payne, Heather; Blott, Jonathan;
        Marshall, Chloë R.; MacSweeney, Mairéad: Language lateralization
        of hearing native signers : a functional transcranial Doppler sonog-
        raphy (fTCD) study of speech and sign production. – *B&L* 151, 2015,
        23-34.

9.4.2.   LANGUAGE DISORDERS

1041   Orie, Ọlanikẹ Ọla: *Acquisition reversal : the effects of postlingual
        deafness in Yoruba.* – Berlin : De Gruyter Mouton, 2012. – xi, 281 p. –
        (Studies on language acquisition ; 47).

9.4.2.2.   APHASIA

1042   Patil, Gouri Shanker; Rangasayee, R.; Mukundan, Geetha: Non-fluent
        aphasia in deaf user of Indian Sign Language : a case study. – *CognLS*
        1/1, 2014, 147-153.

1055 Fischer, Susan D.; Gong, Qunhu: Variation in East Asian sign language structures. – (218), 499-518.

1056 Fontana, Sabina; Corazza, Serena; Boyes Braem, Penny; Volterra, Virginia: Language research and language community change : Italian Sign Language, 1981-2013. – *SLStud* 17/3, 2017, 363-398 | E. ab.

1057 Geraci, Carlo; Battaglia, Katia; Cardinaletti, Anna; Cecchetto, Carlo; Donati, Caterina; Giudice, Serena; Mereghetti, Emiliano: The LIS corpus project : a discussion of sociolinguistic variation in the lexicon. – *SLStud* 11/4, 2011, 528-574 | *LIS = Lingua dei Segni Italiana* (Italian Sign Language).

1058 Geraci, Carlo; Bayley, Robert; Cardinaletti, Anna; Cecchetto, Carlo; Donati, Caterina: Variation in Italian Sign Language (LIS) : the case of *wh*-signs. – *Linguistics* 53/1, 2015, 125-151.

1059 Ghari, Zohreh: Variations in the Baghcheban manual alphabet in Iranian Sign Language. – *SLStud* 18/1, 2017, 73-129 | E. ab.

1060 Hakamura, Naoja: K probleme žestovogo jazyka v istoričeskom kontekste SSSR 30 godov XX veka. – *JSEES* 32, 2012, 141-170 | Jap. & E. ab.: The problem posed by sign language in the historical context of the USSR in 1930s : the educational and employment policy toward people with disabilities and All-Russian Society of Deaf.

1061 Hoffmann-Dilloway, Erika: Metasemiotic regimentation in the standardization of Nepali Sign Language. – *JLA* 18/2, 2008, 192-213.

1062 Hoffmann-Dilloway, Erika: Ordering burgers, reordering relations : gestural interactions between hearing and d/Deaf Nepalis. – *Pragmatics* 21/3, 2011, 373-391.

1063 Hoffmann-Dilloway, Erika: *Signing and belonging in Nepal.* – Washington, D.C. : Gallaudet UP., 2016. – 176 p.

1064 İlkbaşaran, Deniz: Türkiye'deki sağır gençlerin iletişim alışkanlıkları ve Türk İşaret Dili'nin toplumsal dilbilimi açısından incelenmesi. – (615), 411-443 | [Communication patterns among Turkish deaf young people and sociolinguistic research on Turkish Sign Language].

1065 Jónsson, Jóhannes Gísli; Brynjólfsdóttir, Elísa Guðrún; Sverrisdóttir, Rannveig: Variation in wh-questions in Icelandic Sign Language. – (11), 145-156.

1066 Khanal, Upendra: Age-related sociolinguistic variation in sign languages, with particular reference to Nepali sign language. – *NepL* 28, 2013, 64-70.

1067 Kisch, Shifra: Demarcating generations of signers in the dynamic sociolinguistic landscape of a shared sign-language : the case of the Al-Sayyid Bedouin. – (1047), 87-126.

1068   Lucas, Ceil; Bayley, Robert: Variation in sign languages : recent research on ASL and beyond. – *Compass* 5/9, 2011, 677-690.

1069   McKee, David; [McKee, Rachel M Locker] McKee, Rachel; Major, George: Numeral variation in New Zealand Sign Language. – *SLStud* 12/1, 2011, 72-97 | E. ab.

1070   [McKee, Rachel M Locker] McKee, Rachel; McKee, David: Old signs, new signs, whose signs? : sociolinguistic variation in the NZSL lexicon. – *SLStud* 11/4, 2011, 485-527 | E. ab.

1071   Meir, Irit; Israel, Assaf; Sandler, Wendy; Padden, Carol A.; Aronoff, Mark: The influence of community on language structure : evidence from two young sign languages. – *LV* 12/2, 2012, 247-291.

1072   Nonaka, Angela M.: Estimating size, scope, and membership of the speech/sign communities of undocumented indigenous/village sign languages : the Ban Khor case study. – *L&C* 29/3, 2009, 210-229.

1073   Nyst, Victoria: The sign language situation in Mali. – *SLStud* 15/2, 2015, 126-150 | E. ab.

1074   Parks, Elizabeth S.; Parks, Jason: A sociolinguistic profile of the Peruvian deaf community. – *SLStud* 10/4, 2010, 409-441.

1075   [Power, Desmond John] Power, Des: Australian Aboriginal deaf people and Aboriginal sign language. – *SLStud* 13/2, 2013, 264-277 | E. ab.

1076   Quinn, Gary: Schoolization : an account of the origins of regional variation in British Sign Language. – *SLStud* 10/4, 2010, 476-501.

1077   Raanes, Eli: Døve på slutten av 1800-tallet : en språklig og kulturell gruppering? – *MM* 1, 2013, 84-118.

1078   Sande, Inge van de; Crasborn, Onno A.: Lexically bound mouth actions in Sign Language of the Netherlands : a comparison between different registers and age groups. – *LIN* 26, 2009, 78-90.

1079   Schembri, Adam C.; Cormier, Kearsy; Johnston, Trevor; McKee, David; McKee, Rachel M. Locker; Woll, Bencie: Sociolinguistic variation in British, Australian and New Zealand Sign Languages. – (218), 476-498.

1080   Schembri, Adam C.; McKee, David; McKee, Rachel M. Locker; Pivac, Sara; Johnston, Trevor; Goswell, Della: Phonological variation and change in Australian and New Zealand Sign Languages : the location variable. – *LVC* 21/2, 2009, 193-231.

1081   Schermer, Trude: Language variation and standardisation. – (633), 279-298.

1082   Siu, Wai Yan Rebecca: Location variation in Hong Kong Sign Language (HKSL). – *APLV* 2/1, 2016, 4-47 | E. ab.

1083 Stamp, Rose; Schembri, Adam C.; Fenlon, Jordan; Rentelis, Ramas: Sociolinguistic variation and change in British Sign Language number signs : evidence of leveling? – *SLStud* 15/2, 2015, 151-181 | E. ab.

1084 Sze, Felix Yim Binh; Lo, Connie; Lo, Lisa; Chu, Kenny: Historical development of Hong Kong Sign Language. – *SLStud* 13/2, 2013, 155-185 | E. ab.

1085 Tagarelli De Monte, Maria: La scrittura online di sordi profondi preverbali segnanti LIS : semplificazione e interferenze linguistiche. – *SILTA* 44/3, 2015, 532-545 | [The online writing of profound pre-verbal deaf subjects signing ISL : linguistic simplifications and interferences] | E. ab.

1086 Tamene, Eyasu Hailu: Language use in Ethiopian Sign Language. – *SLStud* 16/3, 2016, 307-329 | E. ab.

1087 Vasishta, Madan M.: Social situations and the education of deaf children in India. – (203), 9 p. | Cf. 1152.

1088 Vermeerbergen, Myriam; Nijen Twilhaar, Jan; Herreweghe, Mieke Van: Variation between and within Sign Language of the Netherlands and Flemish Sign Language. – (193), 680-699.

1089 Vos, Connie de: Sampling shared sign languages. – *SLStud* 16/2, 2016, 204-226 | E. ab.

1090 Whynot, Lori A.: *Understanding International Sign : a sociolinguistic study.* – Washington, D.C. : Gallaudet UP., 2017. – 376 p. – (Sociolinguistics in deaf communities ; 22).

10.1.1.   LANGUAGE ATTITUDES AND SOCIAL IDENTITY

1091 Cooper, Audrey C.; Nguyễn, Trần Thủy Tiên: Signed language community-researcher collaboration in Việt Nam : challenging language ideologies, creating social change. – *JLA* 25/2, 2015, 105-127 | E. & Viet. ab.

1092 Fontana, Sabina; Corazza, Serena; Boyes Braem, Penny; Volterra, Virginia: Language research and language community change : Italian Sign Language 1981–2013. – *IJSL* 236, 2015, 1-30.

1093 Herreweghe, Mieke Van; Vandemeulebroucke, Eva: Vlaamse gebarentaligen en standaard Vlaamse Gebarentaal : verstoten of omarmen? – *TeT* 68/2, 2016, 201-236 | Flemish Signers and Standard Flemish Sign Language : embraced or dismissed? | E. ab.

1094 Hoffmann-Dilloway, Erika: Lending a hand : competence through cooperation in Nepal's Deaf associations. – *LiS* 40/3, 2011, 285-306.

1095 Holten, Sonja Myhre; Lønning, Hege R.: Døves språkholdninger
      og norsk tegnspråk. – *NLT* 29/1, 2011, 7-24 | On lg. attitudes towards
      Norwegian Sign Language & Signed Norwegian | E. ab.

1096 Krausneker, Verena: Language use and awareness of deaf and hearing
      children in a bilingual setting. – (412), 195-221.

1097 Kusters, Annelies: Language ideologies in the shared signing commu-
      nity of Adamorobe. – *LiS* 43/2, 2014, 139-158 | E. ab.

1098 Mizak, Marcin: Sign language : a real and natural language. – *LMNf* 35,
      2011, 50-67 | E. ab.

1099 Moges, Rezenet: Dichotomy of the Deaf community in Eritrea. – (18),
      635-639 | On Eritrean Sign Language.

1100 Parks, Elizabeth S.: Identifying overlapping language communities :
      the case of Chiriquí and Panamanian signed languages. – *Multilingua*
      35/3, 2016, 305-330 | E. ab.

1101 Stander, Marga; McIlroy, Guy: Language and culture in the Deaf com-
      munity : a case study in a South African special school. – *PerLinguam*
      33/1, 2017, 83-99 | E. ab.

1102 [Wrzesniewska,   Marta]   Wrześniewska-Pietrzak,   Marta;   Ruta,
      Karolina: Jakim językiem mówią głusi? – język migowy i polszczyzna
      w wypowiedziach głuchych. – *RHKUL* 63/6, 2015, 193-212 | How do
      hearing impaired people in Poland communicate? : the axiology of
      Polish Sign Language and Polish spoken language in the written texts
      of hearing impaired people | Pol. & E. ab.

10.1.2. LANGUAGE POLICY AND LANGUAGE PLANNING

1103 Behares, Luis Ernesto; Brovetto, Claudia; Peluso Crespi, Leonardo:
      Language policies in Uruguay and Uruguayan Sign Language (LSU).
      – *SLStud* 12/4, 2012, 519-542 | E. ab.

1104 Bergman, Brita; Engberg-Pedersen, Elisabeth: Transmission of sign
      languages in the Nordic countries. – (218), 74-94.

1105 Boyes Braem, Penny; Rathmann, Christian: Transmission of sign lan-
      guages in Northern Europe. – (218), 19-45.

1106 Bres, Julia de: The hierarchy of minority languages in New Zealand. –
      JMMD 36/7, 2015, 677-693.

1107 Cabeza Pereiro, Carmen; Ramallo, Fernando F.: Lenguas de signos
      y educación en España : una aproximación desde la comunidad
      sorda. – *LPLP* 40/1, 2016, 1-25 | Sign language in Spain : an approxima-
      tion of the deaf community | Sp., E. & Esperanto ab.

1108   Geraci, Carlo: Language policy and planning : the case of Italian Sign Language. – *SLStud* 12/4, 2012, 494-518 | E. ab.

1109   González Abelaira, Cristina: Unha lingua de signos galega? – *EdLG* 8, 2016, 89-106 | A Galician sign language? | E. & Galician ab.

1110   Gras, Victòria: Can signed language be planned? : implications for interpretation in Spain. – (412), 165-193.

1111   Hermans, Daan; Ormel, Ellen; Knoors, Harry: On the relation between the signing and reading skills of deaf bilinguals. – *IJBEB* 13/2, 2010, 187-199.

1112   Herreweghe, Mieke Van; Vermeerbergen, Myriam: Flemish Sign Language standardisation. – *CILP* 10/3, 2009, 308-326.

1113   Hosoya, Miyoko: Kokugo kyōkasho ni okeru 'shuwa' no atsu-kawarekata. – *ShK* 23, 2014, 43-56 | The presentation of "sign language" in Japanese language textbooks.

1114   Hoyer, Karin: Normeringen av de tecknade språken i Finland : en historisk tillbakablick. – *SpriN* 2010, 65-80 | Standardization of the sign languages in Finland : a historical review | E. & Sw. ab.

1115   Hult, Francis M.; Compton, Sarah E.: Deaf education policy as language policy : a comparative analysis of Sweden and the United States. – *SLStud* 12/4, 2012, 602-620 | E. ab.

1116   Jones, Jill: Towards language planning for sign languages : measuring endangerment and the treatment of British Sign Language. – (175), 87-114.

1117   Kadenge, Maxwell; Mugari, Victor: The current politics of African languages in Zimbabwe. – *PerLinguam* 31/2, 2015, 21-34 | E. ab.

1118   Kanazawa, Takayuki: Shuwa kanren jōrei ga hatasu yakuwari ni kansuru kōsatsu : jōtei purosesu e no tōjisha kan'yo no arikata. – *ShK* 23, 2014, 31-42 | The role of sign language regulations : current state of the involvement of deaf people in the submission process.

1119   Kristinsson, Ari Páll: Vandað, einfalt og skýrt. – *ÍMAM* 36, 2014, 123-126 | E. ab.: Good, simple and clear.

1120   Kubus, Okan; İlkbaşaran, Deniz; Kieran, Shane: Türkiye'de işaret dili planlaması ve Türk İşaret Dili'nin yasal durumu. – (615), 23-50 | [Language planning and legal status of the sign language in Turkey].

1121   Lin, Christina Mien-Chun; Gerner de García, Barbara; [Chen, Deborah] Chen Pichler, Deborah: Standardizing Chinese Sign Language for use in post-secondary education. – *CILP* 10/3, 2009, 327-337.

1122   Lule, Dorothy; Wallin, Lars: Transmission of sign languages in Africa. – (218), 113-130.

1123 Lyxell, Tommy: Färre förskolor för teckenspråkiga barn. – *SpriN* 2012, 73-85 | Fewer preschools for sign language children | On the access to Swedish Sign Language by deaf or hearing impaired children | E. & Sw. ab.

1124 Mann, Wolfgang; Marshall, Chloë R.: Building an *assessment use argument* for sign language : the BSL nonsense sign repetition test. – *IJBEB* 13/2, 2010, 243-258.

1125 Massone, María Ignacia: Ideological signs in deaf education discourse. – (412), 277-295.

1126 Matlosa, Lits'episo: Language policy and literacy among deaf people in Lesotho. – *SAfrJAL* 30/1, 2010, 72-78.

1127 McKee, Rachel M. Locker; Manning, Victoria: Evaluating effects of language recognition on language rights and the vitality of New Zealand Sign Language. – *SLStud* 15/4, 2015, 473-497 | E. ab.

1128 Menéndez, Bruno: Cross-modal bilingualism : language contact as evidence of linguistic transfer in sign bilingual education. – *IJBEB* 13/2, 2010, 201-223.

1129 Meulder, Maartje De: A barking dog that never bites? : the British Sign Language (Scotland) bill. – *SLStud* 15/4, 2015, 446-472 | E. ab.

1130 Meulder, Maartje De: The influence of deaf people's dual category status on sign language planning : the British Sign Language (Scotland) Act (2015). – *CILP* 18/2, 2017, 215-232 | E. ab.

1131 Morales López, Esperanza: Sign bilingualism in Spanish deaf education. – (412), 223-276.

1132 Morgan, Ruth; Glaser, Meryl; Magongwa, Lucas: Constructing and rolling out the new South African Sign Language (SASL) curriculum : reflexive critique. – *PerLinguam* 32/2, 2016, 15-29 | E. ab.

1133 Mori, Sōya: Pluralization : an alternative to the existing hegemony in JSL. – (203), 8 p. | Cf. 1135.

1134 Müller de Quadros, Ronice: Linguistic policies, linguistic planning, and Brazilian Sign Language in Brazil. – *SLStud* 12/4, 2012, 543-564 | E. ab.

1135 Nakamura, Karen: The language politics of Japanese Sign Language (Nihon Shuwa). – (203), 22 p. | Cf. 1133.

1136 Napier, Jemina; Major, George; Ferrara, Lindsay; Johnston, Trevor: Medical Signbank as a model for sign language planning? : a review of community engagement. – *CILP* 16/3, 2015, 279-295.

1137 Nkolola-Wakumelo, Mildred; Manyando, Mulonda: A situational analysis of the use of sign language in the education of the Deaf in

Zambia : a case of Magwero and St Joseph's schools for the Deaf. – *LM* 44/3, 2013, 69-88 | E. ab.

1138 Parisot, Anne-Marie; Rinfret, Julie: Recognition of Langue des Signes Québécoise in Eastern Canada. – *SLStud* 12/4, 2012, 583-601 | E. ab.

1139 Quer, Josep: Legal pathways to the recognition of sign languages : a comparison of the Catalan and Spanish Sign Language acts. – *SLStud* 12/4, 2012, 565-582 | E. ab.

1140 Quer, Josep; Mazzoni, Laura: Transmission of sign languages in Mediterranean Europe. – (218), 95-112.

1141 Quer, Josep: Els projectes de codificació de la llengua de signes cata-lana (LSC). – *ER* 39, 2017, 445-452 | [Codification projects of Catalan sign language (LSC)].

1142 Ramsey, Claire; Quinto-Pozos, David: Transmission of sign languages in Latin America. – (218), 46-73.

1143 Reagan, Timothy G.: South African Sign Language and language-in-education policy in South Africa. – *SPIL* 38, 2008, 165-190.

1144 Reffell, Hayley; McKee, Rachel M. Locker: Motives and outcomes of New Zealand Sign Language legislation : a comparative study between New Zealand and Finland. – *CILP* 10/3, 2009, 272-292.

1145 Schermer, Trude: Sign language planning in the Netherlands between 1980 and 2010. – *SLStud* 12/4, 2012, 467-493 | E. ab.

1146 Sugimoto, Atsubumi: Nihon ni okeru gengoken no hōseika o meguru sho mondai no kōsatsu : kenpōgakuteki na kenchi kara. – *ShK* 23, 2014, 3-10 | Movement to legislate language and linguistic rights in Japan : a constitutional study.

1147 Svartholm, Kristina: Bilingual education for deaf children in Sweden. – *IJBEB* 13/2, 2010, 159-174.

1148 Swanwick, Ruth: Policy and practice in sign bilingual educa-tion : development, challenges and directions. – *IJBEB* 13/2, 2010, 147-158.

1149 Tamon, Hiroshi: Shuwa gengohō no hōseika o meguru kōsatsu : jinken yōgo to no kanren kara. – *ShK* 23, 2014, 11-30 | A discussion on the legislation of the Japanese sign language act : in view of human rights.

1150 Wojda, Piotr: Transmission of Polish sign systems. – (218), 131-147.

1151 Yang, Jun Hui: Sign language and oral/written language in deaf educa-tion in China. – (412), 297-331.

1152 Yang, Jun Hui: Social situations and the education of deaf children in China. – (203), 15 p. | Cf. 1087.

10.1.4.   LANGUAGE LOSS AND MAINTENANCE

1153 Davis, Jeffrey E.: The linguistic vitality of American Indian Sign
      Language : endangered, yet not vanished. – *SLStud* 16/4, 2016, 535-562
      | E. ab.
1154 Hofer, Theresia: Is Lhasa Tibetan Sign Language emerging, endan-
      gered, or both? – *IJSL* 245, 2017, 113-145 | E. ab.
1155 Lanesman, Sara; Meir, Irit: The survival of Algerian Jewish Sign
      Language alongside Israeli Sign Language in Israel. – (1047), 153-180.
1156 [McKee, Rachel M Locker] McKee, Rachel: Assessing the vitality of
      New Zealand Sign Language. – *SLStud* 17/3, 2017, 322-362 | E. ab.
1157 Nonaka, Angela M.: (Almost) everyone here spoke Ban Khor Sign
      Language — until they started using TSL : language shift and endan-
      germent of a Thai village sign language. – *L&C* 38, 2014, 54-72.
1158 Nonaka, Angela M.: Language ecological change in Ban Khor,
      Thailand : an ethnographic endangerment. – (1047), 277-312.
1159 Rarrick, Samantha; Wilson, Brittany: Documenting Hawai'i's sign lan-
      guages. – *LDC* 10, 2016, 337-346 | E. ab.
1160 Wrobel, Ulrike Rosa: German Sign Language (DGS) as an instance of
      an endangered language? – *JLIPP* 3, 2014, 27-37.

10.2.   MULTILINGUALISM, LANGUAGE CONTACT

1161 Kusters, Annelies: Gesture-based customer interactions : deaf and
      hearing Mumbaikars' multimodal and metrolingual practices. – *IJM*
      14/3, 2017, 283-302 | E. ab.

10.2.1.   MULTILINGUALISM

1162 Branchini, Chiara: Fenomeni di simultaneità negli enunciati mistilin-
      gui : bilingui e bimodali a confronto. – (621), 219-236.
1163 Volpato, Francesca: Clitic pronouns and past participle agreement in
      Italian in three hearing impaired bilinguals Italian/LIS. – *RdL* 20/2,
      2008, 309-345.

10.2.3.   LANGUAGE CONTACT

1164 Göksel, Aslı; Taşçı, Süleyman S.: Türk İşaret Dili'nde ödünçlemeler. –
      (615), 361-388 | [Loanwords in Turkish Sign Language].

1165   Green, E. Mara: Nepali Sign Language and Nepali : social and linguis-
        tic dimensions of a case of inter-modal language contact. – *BLS* 35S,
        2009 (2010), 12-23.

1166   Le Guen, Olivier: An exploration in the domain of time : from Yucatec
        Maya time gestures to Yucatec Maya Sign Language time signs. –
        (1047), 209-250.

1167   Mohr, Susanne: The visual-gestural modality and beyond : mouthings
        as a language contact phenomenon in Irish Sign Language. – *SLLing*
        15/2, 2012, 185-211.

1168   Orie, Ọlanikẹ Ọla: From conventional gestures to sign language : the
        case of Yoruba Sign Language. – (27), 244-251 | Also freely available
        online.

1169   Quinto-Pozos, David: Sign language contact and interference : ASL
        and LSM. – *LiS* 37/2, 2008, 161-189 | ASL = American Sign Language;
        LSM = Mexican Sign Language.

1170   Schermer, Trude; Pfau, Roland: Language contact and change. – (633),
        299-324.

1171   Schuit, Joke: Signing in the Arctic : external influences on Inuit Sign
        Language. – (1047), 181-208.

1172   Zeshan, Ulrike; Panda, Sibaji: Two languages at hand : code-switching
        in bilingual deaf signers. – *SLLing* 18/1, 2015, 90-131.

10.4.   DIALECTOLOGY

1173   Eichmann, Hanna; Rosenstock, Rachel: Regional variation in German
        Sign Language : the role of schools (re-)visited. – *SLStud* 14/2, 2014,
        175-202 | E. ab.

1174   Johnson, Russell J.; Johnson, Jane E.: Distinction between West Bengal
        Sign Language and Indian Sign Language based on statistical assess-
        ment. – *SLStud* 16/4, 2016, 473-499 | E. ab.

11.   COMPARATIVE LINGUISTICS

1175   Sze, Felix Yim Binh; Isma, Silva; Suwiryo, Adhika Irlang; Wijaya, Laura
        Lesmana; Bharato, Adhi Kusumo; Satryawan, Iwan: Differentiating
        'dialect' and 'language' in sign languages : a case study of two signing
        varieties in Indonesia. – *APLV* 1/2, 2015, 190-219 | E. & Indonesian ab.

1176   Al-Fityani, Kinda; Padden, Carol A.: Sign languages in the Arab
        world. – (218), 433-450.

1177   Aldersson, Russell R.; McEntee-Atalianis, Lisa J.: A lexical comparison
       of signs from Icelandic and Danish sign languages. – *SLStud* 9/1, 2008,
       33-44.
1178   Minoura, Nobukatsu: A preliminary comparative study of Norwegian
       Sign Language and Malagasy Sign Language. – *TGDR* 88, 2014, 91-116 |
       Jap. & E. ab.
1179   Miyamoto, Ritsuko; Mori, Sōya: Is Kenyan Sign Language a sister lan-
       guage of ASL? : an analysis of language nativity through comparison
       between KSL and ASL. – *ShK* 24, 2016, 17-30 | E. ab.
1180   Sáfár, Anna; Kimmel'man, Vadim I.: Weak hand holds in two sign lan-
       guages and two genres. – *SLLing* 18/2, 2015, 205-237.
1181   Sáfár, Anna; Meurant, Laurence; Haesenne, Thierry; Nauta, Ellen;
       Weerdt, Danny De; Ormel, Ellen: Mutual intelligibility among the sign
       languages of Belgium and the Netherlands. – *Linguistics* 53/2, 2015,
       353-374.

11.1.   HISTORICAL LINGUISTICS AND LANGUAGE CHANGE

1182   Dotter, Franz; Kellett Bidoli, Cynthia J.: The historical relationship
       between Triestine Sign Language and Austrian Sign Language. –
       SLStud 17/2, 2017, 193-221 | E. ab.
1183   Johnston, Trevor; Cresdee, Donovan; Schembri, Adam C.; Woll,
       Bencie: FINISH variation and grammaticalization in a signed lan-
       guage : how far down this well-trodden pathway is Auslan (Australian
       Sign Language)? – *LVC* 27/1, 2015, 117-155.
1184   Kobayashi, Masayuki; Ōsugi, Yutaka: Nyūjīrando shuwa gengohō no
       keisei to hatten. – *ShK* 23, 2014, 57-75 | The development and the pros-
       pects of the New Zealand sign language act.
1185   Kocab, Annemarie; Senghas, Ann; Snedeker, Jesse: The emergence
       of temporal language in Nicaraguan Sign Language. – *Cognition* 156,
       2016, 147-163.
1186   [McKee, Rachel M. Locker] McKee, Rachel: Number, colour and kin-
       ship in New Zealand Sign Language. – (300), 351-384.
1187   Mineiro, Ana; Carmo, Patrícia do; Caroça, Cristina; Moita, Mara;
       Carvalho, Sara; Paço, João; Zaky, Ahmed: Emerging linguistic features
       of Sao Tome and Principe Sign Language. – *SLLing* 20/1, 2017, 109-128 |
       E. ab.
1188   Pfau, Roland; Steinbach, Markus: PERSON climbing up a tree (and
       other adventures in sign language grammaticalization). – *SLLing* 16/2,
       2013, 189-220.

1189   Radutzky, Elena; Canigiani, Elisabetta; Mottinelli, Mauro: Il cambia-
       mento diacronico morfo-fonologico della lingua dei segni italiana. –
       (621), 171-188.

1190   Sagara, Keiko: Nihon shuwa to Taiwan shuwa no goi ni okeru henka
       o saguru : sū no hyōgen o chūshin ni. – *HistLing* 6, 2017, 13-40 |
       Investigation of lexical change in Japanese sign language and Taiwan
       sign language : focus on numeral signs.

1191   Senghas, Ann; Coppola, Marie: Getting to the point : how a simple ges-
       ture became a linguistic element in Nicaraguan signing. – (203), 21 p. |
       Cf. 79.

1192   Taşçı, Süleyman S.: TİD el alfabesinin sözlükselleşmesi ve biçimlenişsel
       yapılandırılması : el değişimi ve benzeşme olguları. – (615), 183-210 |
       Lexicalisation and formalisation in Turkish Sign Language's finger-
       spelling : hand change and analogy.

1193   Wilcox,   Sherman   E.;   Rossini,   Paolo;   Antinoro,   Elena:
       Grammaticalization in sign languages. – (218), 332-354.

11.2.   LINGUISTIC TYPOLOGY, UNIVERSALS OF LANGUAGE

1194   Wilcox, Sherman E.: Symbol and symptom : routes from gesture to
       signed language. – *ARCL* 7, 2009, 89-110 | Case study of the Italian Sign
       Language modal form 'impossible'

1195   Lǐ, Héng; Wú, Líng: Zhōngguó shǒuyǔ yùndòng shìjiàn de cíhuìhuà
       móshì. – *XDW* 36/4, 2013, 355-361 | Motion event integration in
       Chinese sign language | Chin. & E. ab.

1196   Oomen, Marloes; Pfau, Roland: Signing *not* (or not) : a typological per-
       spective on standard negation in Sign Language of the Netherlands.
       – *LT* 21/1, 2017, 1-51 | E. ab.

1197   Rutkowski, Paweł; Łozińska, Sylwia: Argument linearization in a
       three-dimensional grammar : a typological perspective on word order
       in Polish Sign Language (PJM). – *JUL* 17/1, 2016, 109-134 | E. ab.

1198   Schuit, Joke: Signs of the Arctic : typological aspects of Inuit Sign
       Language : (Universiteit van Amsterdam, 2013). – *SLLing* 17/2, 2014,
       276-284 | Diss. ab.

1199   Zeshan, Ulrike; Panda, Sibaji: Reciprocal constructions in Indo-
       Pakistani Sign Language. – (186), 91-113.

12.2.1. CORPUS LINGUISTICS

1200 Barberà, Gemma; Quer, Josep; Frigola, Santiago: Primers passos cap a la documentació de discurs signat : el projecte pilot de constitució del corpus de la llengua de signes catalana. – *TSC* 25, 2015, 287-302 | Cat. & E. ab.: First steps towards the documentation of signed discourse : the pilot project for the creation of the Catalan Sign Language corpus.

1201 Cecchetto, Carlo; Giudice, Serena; Mereghetti, Emiliano: La raccolta del Corpus LIS. – (621), 55-68.

1202 Crasborn, Onno A.; Sáfár, Anna: An annotation scheme to investigate the form and function of hand dominance in the Corpus NGT. – (289), 231-251 | E. ab.

1203 Ebling, Sarah: Building a parallel corpus of German/Swiss German Sign Language train announcements. – *IJCL* 21/1, 2016, 116-129.

1204 Geraci, Carlo: Metodi e strumenti : l'analisi statistica e il software VARBRUL. – (621), 79-94.

1205 Gianfreda, Gabriele: Un corpus di conversazioni in lingua dei segni italiana attraverso videochat : una proposta per la loro trascrizione e analisi. – (621), 95-109.

1206 Johnston, Trevor: From archive to corpus : transcription and annotation in the creation of signed language corpora. – *IJCL* 15/1, 2010, 106-131.

1207 Johnston, Trevor: The reluctant oracle : using strategic annotations to add value to, and extract value from, a signed language corpus. – *Corpora* 9/2, 2014, 155-189.

1208 Lucas, Ceil: Perché usare i corpora nello studio delle lingue dei segni. – (621), 47-54.

1209 Mesch, Johanna; Wallin, Lars: Gloss annotations in the Swedish Sign Language Corpus. – *IJCL* 20/1, 2015, 102-120.

1210 Müller de Quadros, Ronice; Lillo-Martin, Diane C.; [Chen, Deborah] Chen Pichler, Deborah: Methodological considerations for the development and use of sign language acquisition corpora. – (188), 84-102.

1211 Rutkowski, Paweł; Łozińska, Sylwia; Filipczak, Joanna; Łacheta, Joanna; Mostowski, Piotr: Jak powstaje korpus polskiego języka migowego (PJM)? – *Polonica* 33, 2013, 297-308 | E. ab.: The making of Polish Sign Language Corpus.

1212 Santoro, Mirko; Poletti, Fabio: L'annotazione del corpus. – (621), 69-78.

1213   Schembri, Adam C.; Fenlon, Jordan; Rentelis, Ramas; Reynolds, Sally; Cormier, Kearsy: Building the British Sign Language Corpus. – *LDC* 7, 2013, 136-154 | Electronic publ.

12.3.   COMPUTATIONAL LINGUISTICS

1214   Johnston, Trevor; Napier, Jemina: Medical signbank : bringing deaf people and linguists together in the process of language development. – *SLStud* 10/2, 2010, 258-275.

1215   Karpov, Aleksej A.: Komp´juternyj analiz i sintez russkogo žestovogo jazyka. – *VJa* 59/6, 2011, 41-53 | Computer analysis and synthesis of Russian Sign Language.

1216   Maxaroblidze, Tamar: GESL vocabulary and innovation technologies. – (19), 257-266 | E. ab.

1217   Sáfár, Anna; Crasborn, Onno A.: A corpus-based approach to manual simultaneity. – (217), 179-204.

13.1.   ANTHROPONYMY

1218   Borstell, Carl: Types and trends of name signs in the Swedish Sign Language community. – *SKY* 30, 2017, 7-34 | E. ab.

1219   Faltínová, Radka: *Osobní vlastní jména v českém znakovém jazyce.* – Praha : Česká komora tlumočníků znakového jazyka, 2008. – 119 p.

1220   Nonaka, Angela M.; Mesh, Kate; Sagara, Keiko: Signed names in Japanese Sign Language : linguistic and cultural analyses. – *SLStud* 16/1, 2015, 57-85 | E. ab.

1221   Paales, Liina: On the system of person-denoting signs in Estonian Sign Language : Estonian personal name signs. – *SLStud* 10/3, 2010, 317-335.

13.2.   TOPONYMY

1222   Podstolec, Alicja: Nazwy miast w polskim języku migowym. – *PJ* 6, 2010, 80-90 | E. ab.: Names of cities in Polish sign lg.

13.3.   NAME STUDIES OTHER THAN ANTHROPONYMY AND TOPONYMY

1223   Day, Linda; Sutton-Spence, Rachel L.: British sign name customs. – *SLStud* 11/1, 2010, 22-54.

INDEX OF NAMES

This index contains the names of all authors, editors, etc., represented in the main part of this volume. Also included are names of persons who are the main subject of a publication. Names are listed alphabetically by surname.

INDEX OF NAMES

INDEX OF LANGUAGES

INDEX OF SUBJECTS

Printed in the United States
By Bookmasters